T0193264

"WHY GOD?"
BRAVE QUESTIONS THAT NEED
ANSWERS AFTER SUFFERING LOSS

DARREN FRAME

WESTBOW
PRESS®
A DIVISION OF THOMAS NELSON
& ZONDERVAN

WestBow Press books may be ordered through booksellers or by contacting:

WestBow Press
A Division of Thomas Nelson & Zondervan
1663 Liberty Drive
Bloomington, IN 47403
www.westbowpress.com
844-714-3454

ISBN: 978-1-6642-7571-3 (sc)
ISBN: 978-1-6642-7570-6 (hc)
ISBN: 978-1-6642-7572-0 (e)

Library of Congress Control Number: 2022915353

Print information available on the last page.

WestBow Press rev. date: 03/30/2023

It is my hope that this book will speak to you in a meaningful way whatever your current circumstances. If, after you read this, your life has been touched, I would ask you to place this book in the hands of someone else who might benefit from the words on these pages.

Darren

PLAYLIST OF SONGS THAT HAVE SPOKEN TO ME

"You Make Me Brave" - *Bethel Music & Amanda Lindsey*

"Who Am I" - *Casting Crowns*

"Scars In Heaven" - *Casting Crowns*

"Broken Halos" - *Chris Stapleton*

"The Father My Son and the Holy Ghost" - *Craig Morgan*

"Pure Imagination" - *Flannel Graph*

"Walk By Faith" - *Jeremy Camp*

"Eye of the Storm" - *Ryan Stevenson*

"Love Without End" - *George Strait*

"I Still Believe" - *Jeremy Camp*

"Breaking My Fall" - *Jeremy Camp*

"Oceans" - *Hillsong UNITED*

"I Could Sing Of Your Love Forever" - *Sonic Flood*

"The Anchor Holds" - *Ray Boltz*

"Snowbird" - *Anne Murray*

CONTENTS

PURPOSE OF THIS BOOK
- INTRODUCTION

My 20-year-old son Jared died unexpectedly of an infection in 2016. It has taken me several years to reach the point that I even felt comfortable considering writing a book like this one, and once I started, it's been at least another year to complete it. This being my first book, I can say that writing it has been a little like some vacations, ultimately better in the planning and anticipation than the actual execution. In addition, much of the material in this book has come from teaching at grief conferences or other teaching that I've been asked to do, so it didn't originally fit together and wasn't ever intended to become part of a manuscript. Writing a book is hard! That said, I'm assuming if you're reading this, you've likely experienced the loss of a loved one yourself, and if so, I'm sorry. Hopefully, in these pages you'll find answers to the questions that have come to mind since that loss, and most importantly, you'll find some truth that will provide hope for your future. The three following points should give you some background on what I've included in these pages:

1. Many people fall away from God when the unexpected death of a loved one occurs, but interestingly, it is also estimated that

just as many people reach out and find God for the first time or renew a past conviction. This book is designed to answer the difficult "Why God?" questions by giving honest, rational, and spiritual reasons to embrace God rather than run from him.

2. When our faith in God is being tested through the unexpected death of someone close to us, often we find our spiritual foundation isn't as strong as it could be. Bible verses and stories of miracles, including personal platitudes, like "they're in a better place," are often poorly received or can even feel offensive in the moment. For those of us that have dealt with loss, the understandable response can be "Then why didn't I experience a miracle if God is so capable?" or "It certainly doesn't feel to me like they're in a better place!" This book attempts to reset perceptions and expectations about who God really is, what happens in death, and what has really been promised by God when it comes to dealing with suffering and grief.

3. In the most difficult trials, like the death of a child, it is often useful to talk about how we as physical beings can relate to God and let him touch us to begin the healing process. Since unexpected death can often cause us to find ourselves mad at God for letting this awful thing happen, it can make the process of allowing God into our lives in a meaningful way even more difficult. In this book, we'll examine ways that God may have already showed up in your life recently, even though you might not have even realized it!

COMMENTS I'VE RECEIVED FROM OTHERS

* "I don't know how you're making it?" Acquaintance

* "There are two kinds of people ... those that have lost a child and those who haven't. Those who haven't experienced that loss will never truly know what it feels like or what to tell those who have experienced that loss." Pastor

* "I must admit to you, I'm mad at God over the death of your son. I just can't reconcile why that would happen to you and your wife. I can't get past that point in my mind." Friend

* "Your son is looking down on you and he's doing just fine." Friend

* "He's in a better place." Acquaintance

* "Losing your son is awful and it will always be awful." Friend

* "I've prayed and prayed and thought and studied, and I just can't make complete sense out of how God can take children back to himself before he takes their parents." Pastor

1

WHY READ THIS BOOK?

As we navigate life, we have beliefs, and we have actions. When we're children, actions mostly precede beliefs. Children typically act without any deep thought and based mostly on their immediate needs, wants, and desires. To help create more stability in our lives, when we're young we're exposed to teaching, training, and behavior modification techniques designed to cultivate mental discipline to help us restrain our bad behaviors and encourage the good ones. By the time we're adults, the script is flipped so we must first believe something exists before it compels and motivates us to transfer our beliefs into actions.

If you're reading this book, you may have recently had a very painful loss or know someone that has. You may even be in the mental state where you're still having trouble deciphering which direction is up. When we experience loss, it's common to feel confused about a great many things, including even how to act in the moment. Often this foggy existence includes a weird anxiousness as you begin contemplating all the "why" questions about what has just happened to you outwardly, and your heart is screaming for healing, but nothing seems comforting inwardly. C.S. Lewis described the feeling like this: "No one ever told me grief felt so much like fear. I am not afraid, but the sensation of being afraid. The same fluttering in the stomach, same restlessness, the yawning. I keep swallowing." "At other times it feels like being slightly concussed. There is a sort of invisible blanket between the world and me. I find it hard to take in what anyone says. Or perhaps, hard to want to take it in. It is so interesting. Yet I want others about me. I dread the moments when the house is empty. If only they would talk to one another and not to me."

I'm familiar with that feeling from my personal experience since dealing with the passing of my 20-year-old son Jared, which is why I wanted to provide help to others by writing this book. My hope is that the words on these pages will speak to you regarding issues that go beyond just the ones that I've had as a man dealing with the loss of a son. The goal is that the information here helps to touch you in those dark, personal areas where only you have permission to go. Those areas of doubt that you might not talk about with others or even admit exist yourself. I believe that this book holds some information that will get you beyond your pain and that stirs that nagging in your conscience, because the lack of answers can be troubling and can leave you feeling empty and questioning what to believe about God.

As full disclosure, I'm not a Bible scholar or a pastor; however, I've studied lots of material written by people that are, and I've been able to talk with other experts for their guidance. Much of the advice I'm passing along has come directly or indirectly from the works of many credentialed individuals who are qualified to give theological guidance, like Tim Keller, C. S. Lewis, and Philip Yancy, and others. I've also included some specific song lyrics that have come from the playlist of new and older songs that have spoken to me during my difficult days, and that I listed prior to this book's introduction.

My personal background is that I've worked as a full-time college professor at Baylor University and have a successful business I've been part owner of for 30+ years. I certainly don't purport to be the smartest guy in any room, and sometimes I tend to make the mistake of interpreting life more from my own perspective than I probably should. But I can speak to you as a father who unexpectedly lost his 20-year-old son who was just coming into the prime of his life. I'm reaching out through this book because I believe that God is still in control of this world, even though my son unexpectedly died when he was totally healthy just days before. As I've said, the ideas in this book, at least many of the good ones, are not all my own. I've tried to give credit to others whenever and wherever possible, but truthfully, I'm not completely certain anymore which thoughts are mine and which came from someone else's valuable insights along my journey. King Solomon said several thousand years ago in the biblical book of Ecclesiastes 1:9 "there is nothing new under the sun," so from that perspective I only feel blessed to have been exposed to lots of valuable information, been able to sort through it, and to have come up with what I feel are some useful concepts that will resonate with you as well.

As mentioned, as adults we must first believe something before our hearts cause us to be willing to act on that information, allowing us to productively move forward. If you're like me, honest and practical answers for your head are a good start at getting your heart going in the right direction and beginning the healing process.

Believe me, I get it! When you've had a very difficult loss, like the loss of a child, it doesn't take long before you begin to struggle with the very tough questions that arise from your experience. What you probably don't realize is that you've just encountered what are actually the most difficult questions in life, and the ones you never wanted to ask but now feel like you must. What often happens next is that instead of answers to your questions, friends and others begin to try to console you by saying things like "they're in a better place." Although platitudes are at most temporarily comforting but are more likely aggravating as you soon find yourself reasoning that your child isn't supposed to be "in a better place," they're supposed to be right here with you right now!

Possibly the worst part of what feels like the bad dream that has become your reality, is that deep inside, against everything in your being, you may have come to the realization that your loved one isn't coming back, even though your emotions still want you to expect that they might just walk into the room again at any time. As the hours and days go painfully by, little by little the finality of this thing called death begins to become ever more meaningful and real. If you're like me, up until recently, your worldview was that most things in life always had a way of redeeming themselves. If you weren't awarded that job, someone close to you was suffering an illness, or some kind of bad event had occurred, there always seemed to be a hope that the situation would ultimately be rectified with time. Suddenly now, this "death thing" has brought a hauntingly different perspective and a finality that has never been there with most everything else. For me, when this happened the hard questions began to arise like, "Why does God even allow death and how can it be good for anyone?"

When your mind begins to pursue these questions, stories you've heard from others attributing supernatural healing to God, or telling how God continues to do miracles, can be really difficult to hear. Thoughts like these can even seem tormenting because they can make you wonder why, if God could have stopped this tragedy, why didn't He?! I've felt exactly what you're feeling in my own life, and I can say it's a very unenviable place to be because condolences that bring any relief can be hard to find in the moment.

To save you some time, and so that you don't become disappointed with what you're about to read, if what I call 'feel good advice' that's designed to protect your emotions and attempt to provide healing mostly speaks to you, I do understand, but I have to say that this book probably isn't for you. Conversely, if your mind is demanding answers to the very difficult questions about God and death, this book was written with you in mind because I often dive right into difficult situations with some "tough love" advice that's not always what you'd choose but can hold the truth when you can't find it anywhere else. To illustrate, the first tough truth I'll offer you with confidence is that, despite your most sincere desires, there is simply not going to be a person who will walk up to you, or a book you can read, or a place you can go, that will provide you with everything you need to heal your soul from this loss. The reason for this is that, if you're honest, you know that the only thing that could truly "fix" you now is to undo the whole set of events that likely led to your loved one's death. Unfortunately, as far as we know, even Jesus only raised a few people from the dead during his entire ministry on earth, and it certainly wasn't commonplace even at that time. Some additional hard truth is that, despite what it seems like you knew before this event, God never promised to deliver people from bad things while on the earth! To put this in context, all but one of Jesus' own devoted followers, called disciples, were eventually murdered for sticking with their personal convictions and beliefs about their leader. Even the two superstars of the Bible in the New Testament, the apostle Paul, and Jesus himself, suffered terribly for their faith and were put to death as innocent men!

When I say, "tough love," I'm certainly not trying to purposefully be insensitive because I know that you may be feeling worse than you've ever thought you were capable of feeling. I did as well! I'm only feeling obligated to point out these kinds of things because, in times like this, our pain can be multiplying instead of subsiding because our questioning and doubt can turn us from hurting, to angry, and even to bitter. During these times, we must recognize that really bad things can and do happen to "good" people, and that although this idea doesn't seem to square with our vision of who God should be, there is obviously more to that story.

Now what?

Fortunately, it turns out there are *some* answers to those "why?" questions that may now occupy a place at the front and center of our lives. To be completely honest (as I said I would be), not every specific question you may have can be answered while we're on this earth. As a practical matter, the first order of business likely needs to be figuring out how to close up part of that gaping hole that seems like it goes right through the middle of your body (like the sculpture on the cover of this book) and bring some healing to the worst feeling you've probably ever experienced. Thankfully, there is healing available and minor miracles can occur, but it all takes some time. Also, again being honest, the pain will never completely go away (how could it?); but, it does subside. As my wife has told me, she hoped that getting beyond grief was going to be like getting over a bad cold, but, unfortunately, that isn't how it works. The perplexing part of what lies ahead is that the relief you seek doesn't come from inside you. It won't come from pulling yourself up by your bootstraps, or by keeping a stiff upper lip, or just digging deeper into your personal resolve. That statement might be as disappointing as any to some of you who, like me, would prefer to solve our problems by ourselves. Instead, the cure to healing that gigantic, recently opened void seemingly going through you comes from reaching outside yourself and partially by embracing the pain of others.

Although there is a spiritual component to most of what I advocate in this book, I'm not going to say that God is all you need and that if Bible verses don't feel comforting to you at the moment that you're doing it wrong. Unfortunately, if you're like me, while those things may hold the ultimate healing that comes from the pain of losing a loved one, immediately after a traumatic event, they may feel very empty. If you're really struggling after loss, and I know this can be asking a lot, but I recommend that you get yourself at least to the point where you can say, "God, I still believe in you ... but now what?" I realize this can be seriously difficult for some who feel completely abandoned by God in their time of greatest need, and I would never assume that you can just flip a switch in your thinking, because it may take some time. However, if you will VERY SINCERELY go at least as far as acknowledging God is somehow for you and not against you, I will

GUARANTEE that the kind of help you're looking for is available! How about that, a GUARANTEE! Try to get that anywhere else?! The important thing is that you can't waiver in your commitment! Believing that there is a good God and that he's all-powerful, and that he has not lost control of your life or the universe, and that he did see your tragedy just the way you saw it, and that he still does love you, are all mandatory parts of this seemingly peculiar bargain I'm making with you! Again, as tough as committing to these concepts may be, without them, my guarantee won't survive. I hope you're up for this. Do we have a deal?

Now before you begin to think that this book is pedaling snake oil, I'm reconfirming honestly that the whole last paragraph you just read is for real. This book comes with a conditional guarantee for healing!!! Yes! My deal with you is this: I guarantee that the following information will help you to travel the toughest journey you've ever been on; but, your part is critical. Even in deep despair when you feel like you're walking through a long, dark, scary tunnel as I did some years ago, what you must do to begin to turn the tables on your pain is to be honest with your feelings and recognize "Okay, God, I know you're there, but I need you to show me!"

To be clear, I'm not holding myself out as a miracle worker. Nothing could be further from the truth! I only offer you this bargain because I've felt many of the feelings you may be having now. I started traveling down the road a few years ago that still may be ahead of you. The secret behind my confidence is that I know that "all the good stuff"—that can help you out of the state you may be in—is really just hidden in plain sight. Sometimes it just takes some good advice to point the way!

You must remember, I'm not telling you I can bring your loved one back. The last time I checked, and no matter what path you choose to follow going forward from here, no one and nothing can do that! Instead, the place where the healing starts is in YOUR HEAD and in YOUR HEART, in other words your beliefs and your actions, just like I talked about at the beginning of the chapter. The bottom line is that you're the person whom God has left here on this earth, and I think you know that you are still here for a reason.

There are lots of helpful suggestions to aid in your healing that I'll be talking about later in this book, but since we all like instant results when we can get them, and so you won't put this book down because it sounds too outlandish to be true, let me give you a brief example of some help that can begin immediately. I've already mentioned that looking outside of yourself is what I've found is the key to healing. With that in mind, consider this perspective. As part of writing this book, I've done a lot of outside research, so understand that some of the things I'll say here go way beyond just my own experience. In my reading, I came across a book (one of many) about suffering that my wife (who often does this sort of thing) gave to a friend of ours who had just received a cancer diagnosis and was about to start a grueling, two-year regime of chemotherapy and stem cell transplants. The book is called *"Notes from the Valley"* by Andy McQuitty, who is a pastor who has personally suffered with colon cancer for many years. In his book, while he does talk about what it feels like to lose loved ones to cancer, his primary focus is for those that currently have cancer and are involved in the awful process of ongoing cancer treatment themselves. Many of his readers are undoubtedly nauseous and physically sick just as he has been day after day. McQuitty talks about being weakened to the point where he couldn't raise his head off the pillow. Many of us have likely heard of and maybe even seen people like this and know the debilitating effects of chemotherapy that he's describing. My point in bringing this to your attention is to cause you to reflect on this difficult reality, and although your heart feels like it may have just been torn from your body, I would tell you that if you still have the blessing of being able to lift your head up in the morning and see your hands in front of your face, you can thank God for something. Even though it may otherwise be a really bad day, you have your health and there is something to be thankful for! I know this analogy may sound unimportant, and the fact is that you probably have LOTS of things to be thankful for in your life, but sometimes in the deepest of valleys, you must find a point of focus and to begin to change your perspective one acknowledged blessing at a time. Before you leave this line of reasoning, you can likely also count the other blessings, like food and shelter, and especially, your friends that may have been around you recently in your sorrow. As you begin to perform this mental exercise, don't be surprised if there comes a small voice inside you that tells you that "God has been with you through your suffering," and that even though there is still going to be some painful rebuilding to do, he's got you! Although losing your loved one was certainly not your choice, and you would trade it away in a second if you could, you may be on your way to finding that there is strength, wisdom, and eternal understanding to be gained from surviving the very worst of situations!

To summarize, in this book I have tried to take on the toughest issues, mostly regarding your belief in God, including the role you think God should have played in your suffering and loss, and to pursue answers to your questions from a Christian perspective by pointing out the best information I've found to help you through the hardest of times. They'll be no wimping out or avoiding the tough questions and they may lead to some tough answers—maybe even some that seem to defy human reasoning. Just the fact that we live in a world that includes time and space, and we're told that God operates with time as a continuum where he can see the start, the finish, and everything between, is part of what makes some things so hard for us to understand. Additionally, the ultimate sovereignty of God, and the fact that he knows and sees all the things that we don't, might be part of the answer. However, don't be discouraged! There are still lots of available rocks that we can turn over to find some satisfying answers that we can know right now. And best of all, there is hope!

Lastly, as I've said, there are truly satisfying "God-things" you can know about this very hard situation that will help you make it through until tomorrow and the day after that. I'm inspired to share with you what I've found because I know that when I didn't have any answers to my many questions about death and dying, it was even more difficult to face my future. Consequently, I've studied what I think are God's responses to difficult circumstances, and I've tried to pass along what God has revealed about death and suffering, while, hopefully, not getting stuck on the things we don't and can't know right now. You might consider the small truths in this book like the steps of a ladder that will help you climb out from a bad place so you can get on with the rest of what God has for you now. This doesn't mean that, like me, you won't find yourself sliding back down into those dark places from time to time because you're angry that you don't have all the answers and the pain of the bad memories comes rushing in. But don't be frustrated, the battle you're facing can only be fought by following the same advice that's on the shampoo bottle. ..." wash, rinse, repeat."

2

JARED'S STORY

I n August 2016, my son Jared was 20 years old when he passed away from massive seizures resulting from strokes and blood clots in his brain. Just days before he had been an extremely healthy, athletic young man mountain biking and planning for his upcoming junior year of college at Baylor University. This is his story.

Jared was born a very healthy baby, but surprisingly was diagnosed with a defective aortic heart valve when he was two months old. Even though the doctors were very concerned at the time, requiring angiograms and echocardiograms with his pediatric cardiologist every few months, no early intervention was necessary, which my wife and I believed resulted from God answering our prayers. As Jared grew into childhood and regular heart monitoring continued, he was still able to play soccer, basketball, baseball, and be as active, if not more, than his peers.

During regular heart exams and a stress test when he was 12

years old, the cardiologists discovered that Jared's heart was working excessively and was not oxygenating his blood as necessary. With further testing, the doctors saw not only his aortic valve narrowing, but something they had never discovered before, a very rare and life-threatening coronary artery defect, that essentially was closing off the blood supply to his heart when he exercised, which could have ended his life with any strenuous activity. At that time, Jared's cardiologist forbade him any physical activity and the decision was eventually made for him to have open-heart surgery with a pediatric cardiology surgical specialist at Stanford Hospital in California, in hopes of addressing the lack of normal blood supply to his heart.

Jared responded well and recovered quickly, having surgery on Good Friday and by Tuesday, the doctors released him to fly home to Scottsdale, Arizona. Within a few months and lots of tests, it was determined that the procedure was successful and that he could play basketball and resume normal activities, along with his regular cardiology exams every few months, which was truly an answer to prayer!

He was very healthy, an excellent student, and became an accomplished high school basketball player, getting some All-State recognitions. He developed a sense of persistence and confidence as he had experienced much adversity with his health during his young life. As my wife and I, and his older brother before him, Jared decided to attend college at Baylor University in Waco, Texas. He worked hard in school and always made time to strenuously work out and eat healthy.

While in college, he began to frequently enjoy mountain biking, which often involved crashes, bumps and scrapes. In July before his junior year at Baylor, he went with his good friend to mountain bike down the ski slopes in Colorado and took a spill that resulted in moderate scrapes on his hips and elbows, and a blow to the head. After a trip to the local urgent care to get checked for concussion, as was normal for him, he took care of the scrapes and bandaged them, with no real worries of serious injury.

The following week back in Scottsdale, Jared developed what seemed to be the flu, high fever, achy legs, terrible headaches, and nausea. When he continued to get worse, he saw our family doctor who did blood cultures, but felt it was a virus or flu. As Jared worsened the next day, we took him to the ER and tests were run for flu as well as X-rays and other tests. He was sent home with a mild antibiotic in case he was suffering some type of tick bite, but the doctor still felt it was viral flu.

As his condition worsened the following day, his cardiologist wanted to see him to make sure his heart had not been affected by whatever was going on in his body. On the way to the office, Jared began to complain of blindness, his speech became slurred, and he was confused. As his lifelong cardiologist evaluated him and the echocardiogram was performed, it was decided he should be taken to the Mayo Clinic Emergency Room, as it appeared he was suffering a stroke. Shortly after arriving there, a call that came from our family physician confirmed from earlier blood tests that there was a strain of staph bacteria in his cultures, which possibly could have come in conjunction with the scrapes from the mountain bike fall.

The next five days were a whirlwind filled with many, many blood tests, x-rays, MRI, CT scans, doctor after team of doctors of cardiology, infectious disease, neurology, neuro-ophthalmology, and others, all trying to figure out the best plan of action to manage the clots of bacteria that had lodged in Jared's narrowed aortic valve and were now breaking off into pieces, causing strokes and damage to Jared's vital organs and throughout his body. His condition was too fragile to allow for the invasive test that was needed to assess the damage fully and the clots deep in his heart. The plan was to do heart surgery as soon as he could tolerate it and air evac him back to Stanford University hospital as soon as he was stable enough, to have his narrowed heart valve taken out and replaced.

However, very early the next morning when the exam was planned to take place, Jared had a massive seizure resulting from strokes and clots to his brain. He lost consciousness and was taken to ICU immediately and eventually into neurosurgery, in hopes of clearing some of the clots and pressure in his brain from the strokes. Following the surgery, the surgeons and doctors were hopeful, but Jared never regained consciousness. Into the night, his intracranial pressure continued to rise, even after the doctors removed the top of his skull. During this time, we as a family agonized like never before. Jonathan Foster describes the feeling in his book, "Where Was God on the Worst Day of My Life." We paced. We prayed. Like slamming on the brakes and the gas pedal at the same time, we cried and attempted to stop crying." Further CT scans were done, and further neurosurgery was considered, but after the results of the CT scan were read, the doctors admitted there was nothing more they could do to save Jared's life. Foster describes this kind of news like this: "Whatever a heart-breaking sounds like … that's what you heard in the room that evening. It was the thud of darkness. Insanity formed a mosh pit in the middle of my family."

In the very early hours of that morning as our family was surrounded by extended family and dear friends, with tears in our eyes, Jared's doctors said this would be his last day. At that point, Jared had no apparent brain function and hadn't since the intracranial pressure had skyrocketed.

The caring doctors and nurses at the Mayo Clinic worked with us to make his last day as comfortable as possible, as we knew our final goodbye to him was coming when they would shut off the respirator in a few short hours. So many of his friends, our dear friends, and extended family never left our side, and we welcomed all of those who wanted to visit Jared's bedside, because we felt that's what he would have wanted, even though we didn't know if he could hear or see anything that was happening.

Jared's last few moments on this earth still resonate with me as a song was played that was a word picture for when Jared might have been seeing as I could imagine him leaving his body and standing before God.

"I stand before you now, the greatness of your renown. I have heard of your majesty and wonder of you, King of Heaven in your melody I bow. As your love in wave after wave, crashes over me, crashes over me. For you are for us, you are not against us, Champion of Heaven you made a way for all to enter in."

"I have heard you calling my name, I have heard the song of love that you sing. So I will let you draw me out beyond the shore to your grace, your grace!" "You made me brave, you called me out beyond the shore into the waves." "You made me brave, no fear can hinder now the promises you made."

*You Make Me Brave - Bethel Music & Amanda Lindsey

As Jared's heart rate began to race and then the nurses began to see his body was succumbing, everyone who was with us gathered around his hospital bed in the ICU. It seemed like we had about 50 people in his small hospital room. His long-time girlfriend who had remained with him and us throughout these hardest days of our lives continued to play the worship playlist on Jared's phone and we gathered close in around him and sang through our tears, knowing he would soon be going to meet Jesus. Soon after, everyone but family left the room and the nurse said it was time, as his breathing had become labored, and his heart rate was now dropping. We hugged our boy tightly one last time and told him to run to Jesus, that we would be ok.

After the doctors removed all the breathing tubes, Jared miraculously struggled to hang on. The nurse asked if there were someone he was waiting for, and we remembered his pediatric cardiologist said he would be there, and another dear friend was flying back to Arizona from vacation in San Diego to hopefully say goodbye. As they both arrived and came in to give Jared one last hug goodbye, it seemed he was at peace as we held his hand, he died.

Jonathan Foster describes this time better than I can: "There is, of course, great bitterness here. I have played and replayed the events of that day and the events of his life a thousand times more. Like an abandoned rental house full of inconsiderate squatters, the memories come and go in the shelter of my mind. They pay no rent. They are noisy. They offer no solace. They leave little behind except the evidence of their search. I hear their voices from time to time, "He was here." "Where is He?" "He's gone!" The voices are shrill. Sometimes my voice joins them. The truth is I am deeply wounded." ('She' has been changed to 'He').

Young Jared enjoying some "Daddy time".

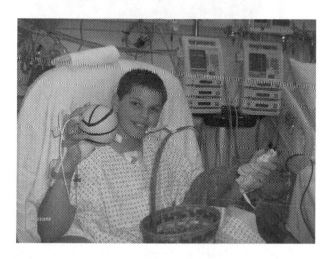

Heart surgery at Stanford Medical Center at 12 years old.

From learning to play basketball at the YMCA.....

To hoops in the big arena and All-State Honors!

Our family Jared's freshman year at Baylor University.

Jared and his girlfriend Lauren.

Jared and his lifelong cardio physician Roy Jedekin.

Jared was an avid mountain biker. Spending time with Dad.

Jared's hopes were to pursue a career in
business and he couldn't wait to start!

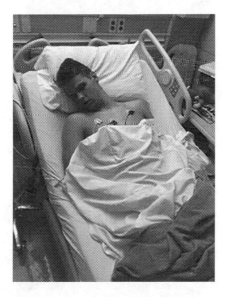

At the Mayo Clinic suffering from a series of unforeseeable issues.

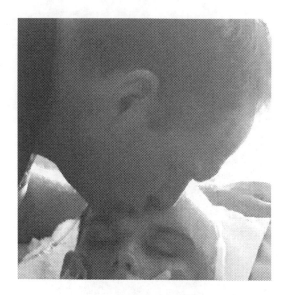

Saying goodbye one last time.

Jared Logan Frame

Celebration of Life
October 25th, 1995 - August 4th, 2016

To be absent from the body is to be...
Present with the Lord.
2 Corinthians 5:8

Celebration of Life program.

3

———— ✥ ————

I WANT SOME ANSWERS!

With the death of a loved one, at times, the visualization can be like sticking your hand through this life and into "the other side of the curtain." You may be able to close your eyes and picture your loved one, or even yourself, stepping out of this life into the next so vividly that it seems like if you reached out, you could touch it. Then, as you try to follow or take the next step, it's as if the door vanishes and you find yourself back in the same spot you started. These kinds of sensations can easily lead you to contemplate the questions of "why me?" or "why God?" and even make you feel entitled to some immediate answers, especially when it's been an unexpected death.

Non-Christians and Christians alike, can't be faulted for wondering where God is in all of this and how could he allow such a terrible thing to happen? This frustration often leads to the logical follow-up question, "If God didn't intervene now in my greatest time of need, was He really ever present in my life or did I get this all wrong?" After my son Jared died, I started down the path of questions that I like to call "mental gymnastics." My thoughts became so knotted-up about God's role in my circumstances that I finally had to say, "God, I'm not going to let myself lose faith in you, but what am I supposed to think now?" Beyond that resolution, my next step was to convince myself, "Okay, Lord, I'm still going to believe you're real; but, where are you now and why didn't you fix this, especially since I and everyone I know prayed that you would save my son, and we prayed really hard?!"

Early in my grief journey when I attempted to describe for people just what it's like to lose a child, I found myself trying to compare the experience to other trials and hardships in life. I soon found that all the comparisons fell short because of one main thing, the permanence of death. In attempting to find something that felt similar to losing a loved one, I realized that often when we pray to God, we're praying that He'll fix something for us or save us from something we don't want to endure. "Fix my body by granting a successful surgery, or fix my frustration by helping me find a new or better job, or help my friend get beyond a troublesome point in life, or find me a way out of this bad situation," etc. However, when someone dies, you realize why Jesus specifically placed so much emphasis in the Bible on defeating death. Death, unlike anything else, has incredible finality that often isn't clear until we lose someone we know well. With death, there is no healing to anticipate, no better job coming on the horizon, and no fixing of the problem. There's no next day or next month when things will finally get back to normal. Until death is so close to you that you can't ignore it or can't dismiss it as someone else's bad fortune, it's easier not to think about because you can convince yourself that it only affects others or that you've been able to avoid it by making smart choices or even just by good luck.

The most disheartening feeling for me associated with the loss of my son was to know that tomorrow wasn't going to bring any new hope and that there wasn't going to be something better coming as it related to him that was going to be different than today. For me, the loss of hope for something better is what separates death from everything else on earth. Often, this time of realization leads people to come to what I call the "Y" in the road of life. One branch of the "Y" says that the God you thought existed wasn't ever real and that you've always just been on your own and didn't know it. This path also leads you to believe that you may have already experienced the best times of your life, and that everything from now on will just be a downhill skid to the finish line. The other path at the "Y" says that there must be something beyond this life. The alternative is a reality that includes a hope for another life that will be most certainly better than this one. This path also includes a plan for the rest of your life here on earth that causes you to desire to remain relevant and fulfill some kind of greater purpose. It also includes hope that, in the next life, you and your loved one will be reunited.

The title of this chapter, I Want Some Answers!, acknowledges that this question can be asked by those deciding to take either path at the "Y," at least initially. It's important to note that for those who thought they believed in God, and even had some idea about what a life after death might look like for themselves, it can still be faith-shattering when they're impacted by the death of someone very close to them, especially if it was unexpected. The foundational understanding that includes what God really says in his Word about death and dying, as well as what He specifically doesn't say, may be put to the test for the first time in people's lives. This foundation should have likely also included some background about what God intends as our true purpose in life while on this earth, and not just the common abstract of "being a good person." I've tried to research both paths people can take at this "Y" in the road and have spent some time thinking about where each path ultimately leads. I believe that there are some things in this book that you may need to know as you reason through some of these issues for yourself.

I am walking a very fine line of outlining what has worked for me and others versus advocating that you follow these directions. As an assertive person, I seldom appreciate when people tell me exactly what to do. As a rule, I like to have some direction from those that I consider knowledgeable, and people I trust, and then decide for myself what seems best for me. However, I will say that in those first few weeks and months after my son died, I felt so lost in the direction my life had just taken, and even though I never felt completely hopeless, I did remember being so emotionally exhausted that I longed for someone to script out for me just what to do and how to react to all the issues swirling around me. As my son lay motionless in the hospital bed, I remember specifically asking a pastor friend of mine, "What do I do now?" and "How do I behave?" There were people all around, friends and family, and I wanted to be cordial and appreciative; yet, I felt completely helpless to know how to fit in, as if I were viewing the whole thing as a scene from my life, as if I were in a movie where nothing seemed real.

This confused and lost feeling is summed up for me so well in the lyrics by Jeremy Camp in his song, "I Still Believe" when he reflects on losing his wife to cancer: *"Scattered words and empty thoughts, seem to pour from my heart. I've never felt so torn before; seems I don't know where to start. But it's now that I feel your grace fall like rain, from every fingertip, washing away my pain. Though the questions fog up my mind, promises I still seem to bare. Even when answers slowly unwind, it's my heart I seek you'll prepare. I still believe in your faithfulness, I still believe in your truth, I still believe in your Holy word, and even when I don't see, I still believe."*

Steve Leder, in his book, More Beautiful Than Before, writes, "The pain you're feeling now may be the first time in your life you've truly felt like you are no longer in control." *That* was certainly true for me. I have been a college-level athlete, earned a master's degree in business administration, been a part of starting a very successful company from scratch, served as a full-time college professor, and have a list of other achievements. Yet when a pastor-friend told me that situations like the loss of a child are even harder for people like me because we're used to doing things our own way, I knew he was right. The idea that it could be dangerous to feel so self-sufficient had occurred to me before, but I had always ignored it and justified my confidence by the fact that my willingness to work harder than most made it all right. Being unable to control a life-or-death outcome, even with the added confidence of being at the Mayo Clinic, one of the best hospitals in the country, was extremely sobering. Even with what I viewed as the "spiritual safety net" of many people praying, and even with many supportive friends around my family and around me, it certainly served as a wake-up call about deciding what I knew or what I thought I knew about this life and about God.

During my son Jared's up-and-down days in the hospital, which included an almost full recovery, and then a tragic and unexpected relapse, I remember being worried about how to deal with the "Why God?" questions that were already coming to my mind. Why had I been subject to watching my son go from the worst, which included a complete loss of vision and cognition, to talking about full recovery and how we would soon be leaving the hospital, to witnessing an unexpected massive brain hemorrhage that would put him in a coma from which he would never recover? Knowing that I wasn't ready to relinquish my faith in God, how could I express what I was feeling without causing me to sound skeptical of God's control and power over the situation, without harming my faith and the faith of others around me? I wanted to believe in God as a loving Father, but I was right in the middle of watching my 20-year-old son die before my eyes. My emotions wrestled with how those two things could both be true at the same time.

During our time in the hospital, there were many friends who had come around to help our family. Some of them had no real faith in God at all, which meant if I questioned God openly with them it would secure the idea for them that belief in God is just a crutch for people who are dealing with personal insecurities. There were others who came with what I would call an undeveloped faith in God, where I knew that the kinds of questions in my head about God would overwhelm their faith because of their spiritual immaturity. And then there were those who came that had very secure faith, and for them I feared my many questions would seem incomprehensible, and that my perceived doubting would indicate that I didn't truly believe in the sovereignty of God.

The truth is that you may come from one of these camps as well. To that, let me say that the questions and insecurities I dealt with and will mention in this book are in no way meant to hurt or offend you, and especially not to endanger your faith. The one thing I can tell you is that the studying I've done in the five plus years since my son died has given me the comfort of discovering that we can all know some of the difficult answers about God's intentions in difficult moments like this, as well as how to deal with the subjects of suffering, grief, and death.

4

———— ✿ ————

I FEEL VERY ALONE!

To dive right into the deep water, it's worth remembering that people have been on this earth for at least several thousand years, and the fact is that many of them, like you, have had to deal with ways to reconcile questions about death, both while believing in God and with no belief! Suffice it to say that through a lot of research, in my opinion, Christianity is the religion that offers the best answers to the difficult "why?" questions. This opinion isn't just because I am a still a Christian and was before I lost my son. To allow you to decide for yourself, the argument goes like this: It's clear and obvious that people who have lost loved ones don't need a belief in God to go on living. However, for those that choose to discard any belief that there is a God that's in control of this world, they must realistically also need to throw out the hope for anything beyond just the world we can see now. By disbelieving in any consciousness of life after death, it's also necessary for these people to relinquish their thoughts of any other-worldly destination for the loved one they've just lost or any chance they'll ever see them again, besides in pictures. So, if you want to assume there is no God and you're completely okay with thinking the one you loved has just gone back to the dust of the earth, okay. But to me, that worldview seems very final and quite hopeless. It also makes a person wonder if the life we're living now, with the kind of pain you may be dealing with from the loss of your loved one, could be the best that things will ever be. Personally, I prefer an option with infinitely more upside! If that sounds attractive to you, and you'd like to believe that you'll be reunited with your loved one again, or even that he or she is "in a better place," those alternatives do come with the prerequisite of believing in God or some kind of supreme being who can make it possible for there to be something beyond our earthly existence.

All this is to say that believing in God is, based on my research, a worthwhile concept to pursue for several reasons if you haven't already, and it can certainly provide you with hope for your lost loved one, if not for yourself. So, if you can bring yourself to say, "Okay, God, I'm confused, but I'm going to pursue you for some answers," and also that, "I'm going to ask for your help and assistance to get me beyond this really bad place that I'm in," you've taken your first step toward a healing process that provides the opportunity for hope and flourishing that includes the time on earth you have left. That's good news!

When I catch myself wondering if I should be putting my faith in a person named Jesus Christ that was on this earth 2,000+ years ago and claimed to be God, I appreciate this excerpt by C.S. Lewis from his book, Mere Christianity: "If a man who was merely a man and said the sort of things Jesus said would not be a great moral teacher. He would be a lunatic – on the level with the man who says he is a poached egg - or else he would be the Devil of Hell. You must make your choice. Either this man was, and is, the Son of God; or else a madman and something worse. You can shut Him up for a fool, you can spit at Him and kill Him as a demon; or you can fall at His feet and call Him Lord and God. But let us not come with any patronizing nonsense about Him being a great human teacher. He has not left that open to us. He did not intend to."

If you've lost a loved one and are dealing with indescribable sorrow, to be fair and honest, you should know that the reason why you can't seem to visualize anything that is going to lift your pain, is because nothing will. If there were something, considering that for millennia people have tried to reconcile death over the years, it wouldn't be a secret and somebody you know would have told you how to do it by now and you'd be on your way to doing just fine! Regrettably, not now, and not ever on this earth will the hurt completely go away! As proof, even just writing this book has caused me to relive some of the events and feelings from my past, and it's still hard for me several years post. But before you quit reading, there are certain truths that have really helped me to get from there to here. One of the stranger truths that may help clear up a nagging question you may have had is to understand that evil is real, and bad things can happen to anyone, and these bad things can be attributed to much of the suffering on this earth. What's most important to know is that the awful things that happen aren't only distributed to generally bad people and not to generally good ones. The point of bringing this to your attention is that what you may be experiencing is not a punishment from God.

Because of your pain, it's easy to understand that your reaction to this statement might be to think, *How can I believe in a God that would allow bad things to happen to good people?* However, if you're like me, chances are you've done plenty of not-so-good (actually bad) things in your life. From hating on people, to lying, or just being difficult to live with, and maybe lots worse. Luckily, when you veered off-course, God didn't use any kind of direct punishment model to zap you with consequences that you may have deserved right then in that moment. Of course, this works in reverse, too. Regrettably, God doesn't always reward you for good things you've done right when you do them, although that would be nice. The problem is, when bad things happen that we didn't deserve, we want fairness, but when we're responsible for the bad stuff, we'd prefer for God to use another standard for behavior reinforcement. We will likely never know, this side of heaven, why God does allow some bad things to happen to generally good people, and why suffering doesn't seem to be handed out proportionately to your actions of good or bad. But based on the fact that we mess up on something nearly every day, the current standard may be better than the alternative!

I'm quite sure I'm not breaking this news to you and that you've had to have realistically known this all along. So, at this point it's good to get past this inconvenient truth and get on to something that can help you heal in the place where you are now. In my experience, to achieve relief that will meet your heart and soul in a place where you need it most in your hardest times, you first must be willing to look beyond this life and, at least one glance at a time, transcend the temptation to make short-term judgments based only on what you see and feel in the moments when you're hurting. It helps to think of this as opening your other set of eyes to view what may have happened in your life from the way that it may be playing out in a more eternal dimension that is far beyond your control and your ability to fully reason.

Let me give you an example. My son Jared was 20 years old and had a very steady girlfriend whom he would likely have married one day in the not-so-distant future. A few years after we lost Jared, she got married to someone else. Think about her trajectory from the 30,000-foot view. What was God's plan for the guy that she married before we lost Jared? What about his family and all the things he will do in his now-married life? I suppose it would be convenient to say, "Well, that isn't my problem," but of course, I didn't have any control over any of this regardless of what I thought about the whole thing or how bitter I could have been toward this marriage. For this event and others, I've needed to resign myself to thinking that, although I would love to have Jared here on earth so that I could enjoy him during the events in what would have been his life, first, it was God's prerogative, for some reason, to take him home to heaven, and second, there are lots of other people and plans God has on this earth that somehow, He wants to fulfill without my boy being in the picture. Again, I'm not telling you that seeing it this way causes the hurt to go away. Of course, it doesn't! But, while Jared and his girlfriend were dating, I came to love her like my daughter that I thought she'd be one day, and at this point I can't allow myself to be so selfish as to say that I don't want the best life for her now. So, even though it's not my first choice, I'm forced to embrace a different picture for her and others whose lives have now changed because of Jared's passing that still can include good things for the people that I love. Through these events, I have to acknowledge that God has unique plans for people I know and don't know, and somehow His plan must have also included taking Jared home exactly when He did.

A song that sums up this feeling is "Walk by Faith" by Jeremy Camp: *"I will walk by faith, even when I cannot see, because this broken road prepares your will for me. I'm broken but I still see your face. You've spoken, pouring your words of grace."*

5

———— ⚜ ————

THIS ISN'T FAIR!

In this chapter, I'm going to suggest to you that even though it didn't feel like it, God may have been right there with you in your difficult times, but that His presence was possibly disguised as the help given to you through your family and friends. If you consider God's presence in that way, you realize he's been looking after you way more often than you thought, although you may still be saying, as I did, "I would trade all of that 'love' from family and friends away just to have my child back," and, of course, you would. No question about it! However, you know that thinking like that has nothing to do with reality, and you also know that in this life things aren't always fair, at least the way fair looks to us. It's okay to think that the price you may have recently paid to gain more awareness of God's love has been incredibly high, because you'd be right. However, in the biggest picture, God is teaching you something through this, and as painful as it may be, you'll only know and understand those hidden blessings months or years from now.

Over time, your recognition of the wisdom you are gaining from the experiences you're having right now will likely completely change your life for the better or for worse, it will be up to you to determine the outcome.

For me, immediately following the loss of my son, Jared, I hit a really low point emotionally and went through some very rocky patches spiritually as I sorted through why I had retained my faith in God but still had so many puzzling questions about His involvement in what had happened. At the worst, my faith journey felt like God had just abandoned me. I wanted hope, but not necessarily righteousness. Of course, what often happens during these rough times is that our thoughts are completely focused on ourselves, and our perspective narrows to the single thought that we've been treated unfairly. In these moments, it's surprisingly easy to be convinced that our hurt is worse than any person ever before, simply due to the pain of the relationship we've lost.

If you flip the script, you know the hardest part about reaching out to comfort a grieving person, even if you would do anything in your power to help them, is knowing what to say and when to say it. We've all been there, longing for the right words, but not wanting to offend. Eager to throw out a lifeline, but unsure if the person really wants to be 'saved' or if you'll just be intruding at that moment. Possibly, right now you're on the other side of receiving and it's hard to remember what a perplexing and awkward situation it can be for others. Understandably, because you feel so drained emotionally, you're not sure what you want, what you need, or if you even care to focus on either. People ask you to let them know if they can do anything for you, and it means almost nothing, regardless of how sincerely they say it. However, even in this strange funk of an existence, you seem to sense that there ought to be something that would help to make this disillusioned existence clear up, but it's equally mirky what that might be. Most likely, you're secretly hoping that if that thing exists, it won't require much effort on your part because you feel you just don't have any energy to spare. However, coming back to reality and putting aside your longing for a "miracle cure" for the moment, chances are that the only thing that helps right now is just the presence of friends and family if you're still near enough to the event that they haven't yet all dispersed. And you should take advantage of that closeness if you can.

For me, as the fog started to lift after a week or two and I started to get the sense of utter misdirection clearing, my attitude got worse as my outlook turned to frustration as reality brought my helplessness into focus. I felt so adrift as I began to wrestle with the lack of answers to the hard questions that were starting now to come into my mind more frequently. The questions were, of course, the why and the how something so awful could happen to me and my family. In that moment, it seems incredibly easy to compare myself to other people who were leading "regular," unaffected lives, and I subconsciously began making a mental list of all the reasons why lots of others deserved to suffer more than I did. All during this time, I kept secretly wanting to believe that there would be someone who would walk up to me and just start revealing all the mysteries of what I just had gone through. But, of course, that day never came.

During suffering, it's incredibly common to say or think that this isn't fair. Of course, the full statement goes something like this: "Why didn't God step into my life during my time of need and save my child? I've always tried to be a good person. I think I deserve that. This isn't fair!"

Tim Keller would describe the sentiments this way, "In our society today, the problem we have is that if we can see no good reason for a particular instance of suffering, God should not have any justifiable reasons either. If evil doesn't make sense to us, well, then evil simply does not make sense."

I can tell you that after all my reading, researching, searching, and studying, starting from the assumption that God is real and that He does care, my main conclusion has been that what I thought I knew about God needed some serious modifications. To avoid the complexities of what can turn into a very intricate theological discussion, the basic answer to the fairness question of why God didn't intervene and make everything right in your life, is that fairness, as we think of it, is not one of the criteria that God uses as He creates the plans of our lives. Additionally, His methods throughout human history have mostly not included simply fixing things just because it seems like He should. I know your reaction is probably *Ugh*, and that maybe I'm either describing a terrible God or possibly that I'm wrong altogether and don't have a clue. But, before you give up, let me explain.

C. S. Lewis addresses what I'm talking about in the Problem of Pain: "The problem of reconciling human suffering with the existence of a God who loves, is only insoluble as long as we attach a trivial meaning to the word 'love,' and look on things as if man were the centre of them. Man is not the centre. God does not exist for the sake of man. Man does not exist for his own sake." "What we hear and now call our 'happiness' is not the end God chiefly has in view:"

In my case, for God to have done what I wished He had done when it came to saving Jared from dying, it would possibly have required an event that went against the laws of nature, or the natural order of things. To be clear, God can and has intervened directly in our world in some circumstances and has saved people in supernatural ways that we would call miracles. We've all seen or heard of them through the course of our lives. Although God does miracles and they can be large and small, history is full of evidence that would tell us that they aren't predictable or normal. Otherwise, they wouldn't be miraculous. What also may have occurred to you is that each one of us has the expectation for a miracle right at the prescribed time when we need it. However, as you study, you'll find that God mostly rejects being available only as the genie in the bottle, which often leads to our frustration. By the way, the difficulty of understanding the timing of miracles isn't a new thing. Even in biblical times, when Jesus walked the earth and did miracles by healing people, He didn't heal everyone he saw, and He didn't do it all the time, and seldom on command. Even Jesus' closest friends were often as confused as we might be about what, when, and why He did and didn't do what was expected.

To unpack this further, there is the sobering fact that all people will ultimately die. The point is that in nearly every instance when someone dies, there are people that are adversely affected by that event. If every person were miraculously saved by God to avoid the suffering of those around them, what would that ultimately look like? I know you're probably thinking that this analogy is way too cold-hearted, and furthermore, that you weren't expecting God to stop all death but only to save just that person whom you knew that wasn't supposed to die. I completely understand, I was too! But there are 7.9 billion people on the planet today and everyone at some point in time is adversely touched by the unexpected death of a loved one or friend, so if the miracles were on-demand, they would quickly add-up. Additionally, if we continue to expect God to do miracles each time they are needed to avoid suffering, we would soon likely begin to want to include other things on the list besides keeping people from dying! Losing a needed job, short- and long-term illness, being unnecessarily hurt by others, etc., all lead to grief in some form. Chances are, during these times, we already call on God to step-in and make things right. So, the dilemma is, should our expectations lead to God, even a God who loves us very much, making all the wrong things in life right all the time? And what if by helping one person, He must hurt another? When you begin to consider our definition of "fair" in this way, as difficult as it can be to hear when we're in pain, expecting and receiving on-demand miracles from God would undoubtedly put our lives into complete chaos. Please understand that I'm not saying that you shouldn't have wanted God to save your loved one, but only to ask you to consider different criteria for evaluating what "fairness" might look like to God, along with possibly altering your personal expectations of how you think He should conduct His business.

I'm truly sorry to take you down this potentially painful road of considerations. Being harsh is not my intention; but, during the tough times when it's easy to be so inwardly focused that our emotions can distort our perspective, it can be worthwhile to consider a new baseline reality. The bottom line is that, with a different focus, we can still view God as good, even though when we cry out with all our hearts, He doesn't always answer the way we think he should.

So, what's the point? What we come to understand is that the way God DOES seem to work in this world is that instead of eliminating events we don't like and that can lead to pain and suffering, in his ultimate wisdom and since He can see all of history from start to finish, His preference is often to support us while we travel through these rough times. Don't get me wrong, I realize your heart is saying you'd prefer He would change His mind on this procedure, at least just this once! Me, too, and amazingly, He actually does intervene upfront at times. I'm sure you won't have to search too far to find someone who's had the good fortune of a miracle, so we know they do happen. However, since I'm not God and you're not either, we can't change what's been done, so it seems that the best use of our time, effort, and emotion, is to try to "fall into" God and allow Him to hold us as He promises He will do. God has also promised that He will never give us more than we can handle with His help, and that He will walk with us through the tough times the entire way. Because, contrary to our wish that God would have done a miracle or handled our situation another way, the absolute truth is that to improve our character, or add to our wisdom, or just to truly understand how to help others when they struggle, God never does promise that He will cause everything to be right for us this side of heaven. What He does commit to is that He will be the one holding the safety net to catch us when we fall, and that He'll hold our hand as we walk back up the stairs of this life.

Chris Stapleton talks about this line of thinking in his song, Broken Halos:

"Broken halos, folded wings that used to fly. They've all gone, where did they go broken halos that used to shine. Don't go looking for the reasons,

don't go asking Jesus why, we're not meant to know the answers, they belong to the by and by."

I realize that although all these things I've just said may sound like a lame attempt to be comforting, they don't really help much when you're in terrible pain. Since you may be hurting really badly along with feeling mentally confused at the moment, let's go back to the thought I mentioned earlier about how you're secretly hoping that some person or something will come along right now and provide some relief. Even if it's just temporarily! Where this emotional state can be so confusing is that there are often many people around in the first few days that ask us what they can do to help. They may say, "if there is anything I can do, let me know," which can strangely even add to your frustration because you don't know what you need! When you're in this position during a quiet moment and are not being put on the spot, I would encourage you to consider what are the things that do provide some comfort and make a written list, or at least mental notes of those things so other people can respond. This exercise will serve two purposes. First, focusing on the relief you've received from others will likely magnify the benefit of whatever those things may be. Second, because of your current experience in dealing with grief, at some point you'll be asked to help others in similar situations, and some helpful suggestions will make you more useful. You may think this is ridiculous since all you really care about now is making it through until tomorrow. But tomorrow will come, and the next day, and the next after that, and when the days turn to months and the months turn to years since your loss, you'll look back and need help remembering the things that made a difference for you in the moment. As a side note, even though you'll always feel this loss, what will likely become apparent in a reasonably short period of time is that you'll be able to look back and see how God was holding on to you through the people that came around you to help!

Here are some ideas to get you started and give you an idea of the kinds of things that other people say have helped them through very hard times. In the book, "More Beautiful Than Before", Steve Leder, a Jewish rabbi, explains what seems to be beneficial coming from the side of the person trying to provide the comfort. He says, the first thing people can do is just to show up ... over and over. The problem when friends say, "call me if you need anything," is that it puts the burden on the suffering person, and most people likely won't call. But, if as the helper, you're available time and time again, people will observe your sincerity and they'll also feel less like it's an imposition to ask you for help as things come up. Also, voluntarily talking about good things or good memories of the person who has passed is never a bad thing to do. Asking the suffering person to tell you about a cherished memory or something about the person who has passed is actually a way to begin healing. Often people think that those in pain don't want to talk about the person who has died, but vocalizing feelings can be very helpful. Notes, cards, and calls mean a lot. Anticipate the needs of people in pain without being asked. Carpool duty, dinner, taking some pressure off at work, going with them to doctor appointments, are all tangible ways to help. Leder also says, "People in pain are worried and they need someone to worry with them. Be willing to listen, no matter how sad it makes you. Listen and be unafraid to talk of death or fear. This is real friendship. This is real love." If you're the one suffering, consider suggesting these things when people want to help, but want to hear from you.

In summary, when you have that thought that God hasn't treated you fairly or that you've been abandoned when you needed Him most, consider this: It's likely that you've believed in God for many years, maybe all your life. For all that time you've certainly known people or known of people, who lost children or loved ones to cancer or various tragedies. Interestingly, during those times you've never likely thought to yourself, "God must not care about those people because their loss doesn't seem fair!" So, why now, only when the tragedy is yours, would you consider that maybe God doesn't exist or isn't a loving God that's active in our lives? Does it make sense that only when it's your problem that God didn't do as requested because He didn't care about you? Tim

Keller says it this way, "We think to ourselves that such things happen to other people, to poor people, or people that don't take precautions." We try to make sense out of things and how they couldn't happen to us.

In your life, when unexplained, good things happened that were beyond your control, did you believe that God was responsible for blessing you. Very possibly! And wasn't it a blessing from God to even allow you to enjoy the time you did have with that child or loved one for the time that you did have with him or her?

If, like me, you expected something from God that seemed of the utmost importance, but didn't receive it as planned, you might realize your view of God has been very conditional. It's very easy to view God as a personal genie that we give hollow acknowledgment in good times, and only pursue with conviction to rescue us from trouble in bad times. The reality is, although God is always there when we call, He doesn't always respond on command or exactly as we'd like. We've probably always realized that God's ways aren't always our ways, but possibly things were never bad enough for us to really put any effort into building our relationship closer with God. Now that the trials have come and God hasn't responded to our pleadings in a way that make sense to us, it may have brought us to a crossroads in our faith. Phillip Yancy summarizes it like this, "The mysteries of time the way God sees time may be the only answer to the question of unfairness. No matter how we rationalize, God will somehow seem unfair from the perspective of a person trapped in time. We remain ignorant of many of the details, not because God enjoys keeping us in the dark, but because we have not the faculties to absorb so much light. At a single glance God knows what the whole world is about and how history will end. Not until history has run its course will we understand how 'all things can work together for good.' Faith means believing in advance what will only make sense in reverse."

These different C. S. Lewis comments paint this picture in all different ways:

"Not that I am (I think) in much danger of ceasing to believe in God.

The real danger is of coming to believe such dreadful things about Him. The conclusion I dread is not 'So there's no God after all,' but 'So this is what God's really like. Deceive yourself no longer."

"My idea of God is not a divine idea. It has to be shattered time after time. He shatters it Himself."

"What do people mean when they say, 'I am not afraid of God because I know He is good?' Have they never even been to a dentist?"

6

———— ❦ ————

WHERE WAS GOD WHEN
I NEEDED HIM?!

It's not difficult to understand why people would say that they lost their faith in God due to the death of a child or loved one. After all, how could a good God possibly allow something as seemingly cruel as for someone to die early in life? After much contemplation about this question, I believe that the way tragedy affects a person's faith boils down to their perception of God, which means what they believe God's obligation is to prevent bad events from happening in their lives. This perception is many times based on what people have been led to believe rather than what God has said about Himself or what He will do. The confusion about who God is and what He has promised also stems from the common assumption that we as humans can really only know about God and not personally know Him, since He isn't an actual person, and since it seems He only interacts with us at arms-length. Tim Keller describes it this way, "You may not feel God in your darkest times, He is still there. We may hear our heart say, 'it's hopeless'. But this is when we must allow our head to say, 'That depends on what you're hoping for.'"

Interestingly, I've had people tell me that by asking, "Why did God allow this to happen?", that I was doubting the sovereignty of God, or potentially accusing God of doing evil. For several reasons, I don't see it that way. After spending quite a bit of time researching the "why God?" question, I'm convinced that God somehow knew exactly what he was doing when he took my 20-year-old son to heaven back in 2016, and also that it was completely part of His plan. However, because I'm not privileged to know or see the whole picture of my life and Jared's, I still can openly admit that I passionately dislike this outcome and I don't expect to change my mind as long as I'm on this side of heaven! I'd even go so far as to say that the events surrounding my son's death still seem to me to be contrary to God's nature, although I'll be very interested to someday find out why that isn't exactly correct! That said, because of the same bargain I've made with you about believing God still loves you, I'm completely admitting that my perspective about who God is must still be lacking, and that in order to be more complete in my faith, I will be in the process of re-learning what I thought I knew for the rest of my natural life!

Because of the pain I've felt as a result of my son's death, you may, like me, be figuratively kicking and screaming about a similar outcome because God is in the process of teaching us to see that our lives on earth are short and very fragile. I find this perspective on life even more confirming because of the era in which this book is being written. Certainly, for me, the COVID-19 pandemic and all the associated restrictions had the same but lesser effect of showing this same truth. What was demonstrated by the mandated lockdowns and isolation, maybe for the first time, was that no matter how much we fancy ourselves as in charge of our lives, we are really not in as much control of our circumstances as we think we are.

Anne Murray talked about this feeling way back in the 1960s in her song, Snowbird:

"Now I find such emptiness within, the thing that I want most in life's the thing that I can't win"

The best analogy I can think of that describes our short-term and long-term relationship with God comes from observing famous people, like celebrities or professional athletes. Seemingly, celebrities have two kinds of friends. The old friends, who they grew up with or that they've known for years and who were around before they rose in popularity. These people are usually called their "inner circle." The other type of friends are what seem to be the "hangers-on," who have come around recently and are most often people who benefit from having a relationship with these famous people. The "hangers-on" often have hollow relationships with the famous person, because as soon as their popularity or money runs out, they frequently leave and are on to the next relationship that can provide something they want. When it comes to our personal relationship with God, if we don't have a well-established relationship with Him, when something happens, like the loss of a child, we can no longer see the value of pursuing spiritual things because they didn't provide the miracle that was expected on our side of the acquaintance, causing us to fall away. Conversely, those people that have made it a priority to have that "inner circle" relationship with God can also find the motivation to remain committed to Him because the basis of their interaction with God wasn't just the personal rewards accumulated for religious activities. Regrettably, if you realize you've been "hanging-on" to God for what you perceive God should have done for you, there's a good chance this might not be entirely your fault. In my observation, because Western culture today has become so incredibly pain-averse, the teaching in many Christian congregations often trends toward what I call the "prosperity gospel." Of course, this is not prosperity at the level of some TV evangelists who preach that God will make you rich and successful, but still churches often manipulate what's taught to create the perception that if you do good things and live right, God will automatically protect you from the bad things and that your respectable behavior will always be rewarded with blessings. While pursuing a virtuous lifestyle is biblical and has lots of sensible merit, the teaching that good behavior leads to smooth sailing in life just doesn't square with what the Bible actually says.

I know this may be a counterintuitive and a tough message about God for some, but as they say, sometimes "desperate times can call for desperate measures," and this may be a good, but difficult, time for you to understand that God has never promised that good works will always reap good rewards while we're on this earth. All that said, when going through the terrible suffering that accompanies the death of a child or a loved one, it's still easy to see how many of us can be disappointed with God. And again, if you're like me, you wish there would have been a better way to understand the finality of death and how to deal with it before having to live through it. Additionally, no matter what your background, it's difficult to see how anyone can make it through something like the loss of a child without thoughts of doubt, frustration, and anger.

As the stark reality of death has swept over me in these times, another somewhat-related thought has come to my mind and that is that I'm certainly not the only person to have walked in these same shoes. Of course, there have been literally millions and millions of people who have lost children or loved ones but for the first time I began to seriously consider how others who have believed in God have dealt with this pain before me. As I mulled this thought over, I found myself thinking that if God is compassionate, he certainly must have left us some tools for dealing with the intense pain, but where are we to look? Additionally, I've reasoned that the path I'm on must be part of a process that leads somewhere. But to where?

Especially in crisis, if we believe in God, it's natural to ask Him to show his power and to save our loved one. Although we hear of miracles and of people being delivered from tragedy, but more often just as when Jesus walked on this earth, God's timing doesn't correspond with our expectations. Although God could change any circumstance at any time, I believe that the reason He doesn't always rescue us on demand is that God desires something from us that a miracle could never achieve. As proof, while the healing miracles done by Jesus and the apostles that are documented in the Bible always worked out well for the recipients, many of those people who directly witnessed these acts firsthand didn't ever undergo a meaningful life change. Significantly, what this leads us to consider is that God desires our free love for him that is not predicated by any on-demand performance, no matter how genuine our desire might be. Because of this, his methods are often intended to solicit a heartfelt devotion to know Him, rather than just an allegiance to pursue His power and capabilities. For instance, we can likely recall times when we've prayed to God for good things to happen, but even when they did, it only took the next challenging situation in life to make us lose sight of God's hand in our last positive outcome. If this scenario describes you, don't feel alone because this just seems to be human nature because people for centuries have had the attitude what-have-you-done-for-me-lately when God's acts of benevolence don't come on time and as soon as requested.

In the first three or four weeks after losing a loved one, it's not uncommon to struggle with how to manage your grief, especially since your routine and perspective have changed so quickly. For the first week or two, it's very likely you've had friends and family around that are not usually around. During this time, the unfamiliarity and confusion of the recent events, mixed with the fact that there are people who love you but aren't usually part of your day-to-day life, may keep you from feeling the full reality of your situation. As things return more closely to normal, although you certainly should make time for personal grieving, I believe that too much unstructured time of reflection can often allow the pain to get ahead of you, which is probably not wise. When I say get ahead of you, I mean that possible downward spiral of thoughts that can take you into a really bad place that you may not have even known existed.

Things I recommend to keep you from sliding too deeply into grief are:

1. Keep reaching out to people who have offered help. Remember, lots of people would do anything to help you but don't want to force themselves on you either. Don't be afraid to schedule a coffee or a lunch or visit with someone every single day.

2. Remember, helping others also affected by this loss will also help you. There are likely many of your friends and family members that are also feeling the pain of this same loss and can probably use your love and support. Reaching out to help others will often temporarily divert your thoughts off your own pain, which can bring welcomed relief.

3. When you do find yourself alone and feel your thoughts start spiraling down, lift your eyes and force yourself to see the bigger picture. Life is short for all of us. This pain will not last forever. If you and the loved one you lost are Christians, the Bible says you will see each other again in heaven. Keep in mind that many of God's promises are ultimately much more focused on the eternal and not the temporal realm of this life. Things obviously don't always go the way we'd like, but we can count on a promise from God that transcends the worst days on earth and that includes better days in heaven than we can currently imagine. In the meantime, God has left us behind on this planet for a reason. We have unfinished business that almost certainly includes reaching out to others who will soon go through the same grief, sorrow, and pain that we are in now, and it may be up to us to assist them in their time of need!

4. Ask "What does God want from me through this" rather than "What do I want from God." This line of thinking, while not always immediately fulfilling, will likely put you on the road to pursuing the kind of truth and meaning that will lead you to healing.

In summary, since I've been exactly where you are, I can understand how easy it is to say to yourself, "I don't see God in this situation, where is He as promised?" The reality is, God has been there with you the whole time. Unfortunately, like a lot of things in this life, it just doesn't look like what you'd expect. However, God has been there with you cleverly disguised as your family and your friends and others who have come to help, and His hand has been reaching out to you in this awful situation. He was there in the form of the medical personnel who may have been involved. He was there when the friends you hadn't heard from in a while reached out and called to tell you they are thinking about you. If you look back with your eyes wide open, you'll see God was there and He's holding you in this very moment because that is how He works!

7

HOW COULD A GOOD GOD
ALLOW THIS KIND OF PAIN?

I f you've recently suffered the pain of losing a loved one, your Christian friends may have told you that you need to rely on God. But what does it mean to "rely on God" or other often-heard recommendations like "God will be there for you?" I must admit that when I was really hurting, certain things people said about God were difficult for me to hear, as I'm the kind of person who struggles with empty promises or cliches from people who don't know what else to say. What I'm going to suggest next may seem just like more well-meaning but practically hollow advice; but, hear me out. The strange reality about God that I feel like I knew before my son died, but probably never really sorted out, is that there are lots of "God-things" that seem counterintuitive and never play themselves out aside from very difficult situations, things that our sensibilities say should be one thing often turn out to be another. For me, the pain and grief of dealing with the loss of my son has included some of those "God things."

What I've discovered, even against my contrarian attitude and much to my amazement, is that when it comes to suffering and grief, the road to healing requires less personal effort than more. My experience has been that instead of shutting others out and trying really hard to work things out myself, I've had to become transparent with my emotions to others to find any relief. As a "type A" personality, my instinct has always been to reach deeper inside myself to find what it takes to meet the next challenge. On this unpleasant journey, certain attempts to deal with my sorrow have worked exactly opposite of my normal approach to overcoming a problem. Not until I allowed my broken spirit to be revealed to others did I begin to find the people and resources that I believe were sent by God to begin to heal me. I realize this sounds like smoke and mirrors, but for me, this is exactly how it worked.

My experience has been reminiscent of the Sonic Flood lyrics from the song, "I Could Sing of Your Love Forever," by Martin Smith: *"Over the mountains and the sea, your river runs with love for me, and I will open up my heart and let the healing set me free."*

The reason why I recommend a strategy that includes becoming more open and vulnerable with such high confidence is because, although I would not consider my experience an exemplary success story in this area, I have seen lots of people who have unsuccessfully tried the opposite approach. When those who have lost loved ones are still struggling deeply long after their loss, I'm convinced that one of the main reasons isn't because God refuses to help them, it's because they won't let Him. Most people would say they want to find relief from their suffering, but many times they're so angry with God, or so proud of their self-sufficiency, that they shut the door of their lives to outsiders. Even more unfortunate is that one of the ways some people continue to keep that door shut and try to deal with the pain themselves is to turn to drugs or alcohol or other addictive, self-destructive choices.

When Jesus was on the earth, He never promised that bad things wouldn't happen to good people. As evidence, really bad things even happened to Him, his close loyal friends, and even to many of his followers. The good news is that after He died, He did say that God's Spirit would be provided to walk with us through the pain that life can bring. To put this to the test, and assuming that some healing might feel good for you right at this moment, one way to see if this is true is to let your guard down long enough to see what happens. The method for doing this is to begin to release the anger and frustration you might be feeling that has resulted because what has happened to you doesn't seem fair. If you will sincerely say, "Here I am God, I believe you can heal me in this damaged state, and I'm going to open my emotions to you," you'll be making a huge start. I realize that doing something like this may feel very foreign to you and it can take all the strength you can possibly muster to become this transparent, you may even feel like you're only talking to yourself. But, if you'll sincerely try, I can guarantee that you'll feel that huge hole that runs right through you begin to close almost immediately and right on the spot. Really!

I'm not telling you it will fully close all at once. Unfortunately, healing, even with God's help, takes time. Lots of time. But remember what I said about Jesus and that His primary promise is that He will be faithful to walk with you and continue patching that enormous, painful void over the rest of your life.

I'm sure, if you're honest, you realize that the feelings of pain and heartache are never going to completely go away, at least, not on this earth. What's interesting is that maybe you really don't even want them to go away. Unfortunately, many of your good memories of your loved one are also those things that keep that wound open and will keep it sensitive going forward. The way this has played out for me since the loss of my son is that those feelings of deep sorrow from losing him are always seemingly right there under the surface. However, what has seemed to happen over time is that the surface just gets thicker and less sensitive. I liken it to a deep cut. Cuts will gradually heal if you take care of them and apply the proper treatment. If you don't, they may get worse and could become infected and harm you from the inside out. Just like a cut, gradually the acute pain in your life will scab over and begin to heal unless you bump the scab. However, there will likely be times where you may rip the scab right off and the wound will bleed all over again. Sooner or later, the cut will become a scar, leaving a permanent mark on your skin. Once the scar forms, only a direct blow, like unexpectedly seeing a picture of the person, or having an unsolicited memory, for example, will bring the acute pain back for a time. Over the years the scar will begin to disappear, but will never be gone completely. My wife and I have met people who lost children 20 years ago or more that will say certain things can still "bump their scar" enough to make them teary about their loss, although the pain usually doesn't last very long.

As your mind begins to clear from the fog, which is a very common description of the feeling people have that have suffered loss, your thoughts will often dart here and there to begin to try to make sense of your new reality. If you have some biblical knowledge or someone around you does, you might have been confronted with the Bible verse Romans 8:28, "God works all things together for good ..." For most people verses like these can seem at best confusing, and at worst downright offensive. After all, what good can possibly come from the loss of a loved one?

In all my reading I found that this often-quoted passage from the apostle Paul should be considered what J.I. Packer calls an "antimony," as described in his book, "Evangelism and the Sovereignty of God". Packer says an antimony is "the contradiction between conclusions which seem equally logical, reasonable or necessary. In other words, something that gives the appearance of contradiction. It is not a real contradiction, though it looks like one. It is an apparent incompatibility between two apparent truths." In the Romans verse, the contradiction is present because even though death is obviously tragic, and death of someone at a young age is clearly not what God has normally planned for children or even adults, even then there can still be some hidden blessing or unseen good that can be a by-product of the tragedy. Interestingly, Packer explains that mysteries like this are not to be confused with paradoxes. As he explains, "A paradox is a figure of speech, a play on words. It is a form of a statement that seems to unite two opposite ideas, or to deny something by the very terms in which it is asserted." The descriptions "service is perfect freedom," "sorrowful yet rejoicing," "having nothing yet possessing all things," and "when I am weak, I am strong" are all paradoxes. Unlike these figures of speech, Romans 8:28 says exactly what it means, however part of the meaning is hidden, making it unique and even perplexing.

As an antimony, the reason this verse is often misunderstood is because our focus is primarily on ourselves and mostly in the present, rather than with what might happen over the course of our lives or in the lives of others. What the verse "God works all things together for good …" doesn't say, but might be implied, is that all things will be "better" without the person that we've lost. For me, I still miss my son terribly and I could never be convinced that his absence from this world was a good thing in-and-of itself. However, the potential "good" still coming from his death might possibly be related to what I do with the rest of my life on the earth, or the "good" his story might be for others who find strength from something I might say and maybe even for you who are reading this book. For people like me, what can happen through the pain of a tragic event like this is that we are often prompted to become kinder and more compassionate toward others because it affords us the capacity to empathize directly with others that are hurting. In my life the proof of all of this came quickly when my wife and I were asked to speak about our loss at our church and at grief conferences for other parents, allowing us to interact with others who had recently experienced loss and needed help. From our firsthand experience, we've realized that we can't "fix" their lives, but that simple acts of service and empathy can be very impactful in easing their pain.

Another example of antimony was demonstrated recently by author Tim Keller, who has written what I think is one of the best books published about all the different grief scenarios, "Walking With God Through Pain and Suffering". Even after writing this book which has helped tens of thousands of others through very difficult problems, the following is what Keller wrote when he himself was diagnosed with pancreatic cancer:

"One of the first things I learned was that religious faith does not automatically provide solace in times of crisis. A belief in God and an afterlife does not become spontaneously comforting and existentially strengthening. Despite my rational, conscious acknowledgment that I would die someday, the shattering reality of a fatal diagnosis provoked a remarkably strong psychological denial of mortality. Instead of acting on Dylan Thomas's advice to 'rage, rage against the dying of the light,' I found myself thinking, What? No! I can't die. That happens to others, but not to me. When I said these outrageous words out loud, I realized that this delusion had been the actual operating principle of my heart."

Keller went on to say, "I spent a lifetime counseling others before my diagnosis. Will I be able to take my own advice?" MARCH 7, 2021, The Atlantic … Growing My Faith in the Face of Death

If you're reading this book, you, like Tim Keller, may have come to realize that things in life are radically different now that you're the one doing the suffering. Even though suffering can lead people toward finding God for the first time, for those of us who have lost children, the price for this enlightenment has been astronomically high, and to be honest, I'm quite certain I wouldn't pay that price if the option were given me beforehand! Maybe that is the reason why God orchestrates events in our lives that are not prerogative! In my case I have felt fortunate that I've been able to rely on the strength and wisdom of others God has put into my life to help keep me from going off the rails in this very turbulent time. I'd encourage you to seek out that kind of help as well!

8

SUFFERING IS WEIRD! (FLOW CHART)

I realize that during suffering, when it comes to our heart and our emotions, we're mostly just longing for something to make the pain go away or even just to divert our attention from it for a time. C. S. Lewis described the feeling this way in the book he wrote about the loss of his wife, "A Grief Observed": "Aren't all these notes the senseless writhing of a man who won't accept the fact that there is nothing we can do with suffering but to suffer it? Who still thinks that there is some device (if only he could find it) which will make pain not be pain? It doesn't really matter whether you grip the arms of the dentist chair or let your hands lie in your lap. The drill drills on." "And grief still feels like fear. Perhaps, more strictly, like suspense. Or like waiting; just hanging about waiting for something to happen."

From my personal experience and from talking to others, grief feels like the experience of being buffeted by waves in the ocean as the painful feelings come and then go. My family has always spent our summer vacations in San Diego, California, and when we're there, we spend much of our time at the beach and swimming in the ocean. It's amazing how the sensation of grief is so very much like the waves in the Pacific that can completely engulf you as you wade into deep water, but then will subside and become less impactful as you reach the shore. What I can tell you is that the waves of grief never completely end, but the waves do seem to grow further apart as time goes by. During those "calm" periods between the waves, being a person who likes to fix things that are broken, I have often found myself wandering around in the philosophical wilderness of "why" questions that seem related to the loss of my son. Two of those questions are "Why does God allow suffering at all?" and "If God can do anything, why doesn't He just not include the bad stuff that doesn't seem to help anyone?" Strangely, I found lots of research on these topics that's given me a different perspective on the waves of grief that I've found still hit my heart from time to time.

"In oceans deep my faith will stand. And I will call upon your name, you keep my eyes above the waves, when oceans rise my soul will rest in your embrace, I am yours and you are mine … My feet may fail when fear surrounds me, you've never failed, and you won't start now." *Oceans – Hillsong United

When we're healthy and things are going well, we often lose sight of how fragile life can be and how quickly things can change. All it takes is a troubling email, a physical movement that leads to unexpected neck or back pain, a car accident or even something much larger like the COVID-19 crisis appearing out of nowhere and changing the entire world. No matter how hard we work to avoid suffering and pain, we are always just inches or moments away from unpleasant circumstances. The interesting thing is that when we look back on our lives, many of these unwanted events and times of struggle have led to what becomes positive changes in our lives. More and more studies by leading psychologists are substantiating the words in the Bible in Romans 5:3 where the apostle Paul wrote that "suffering produces perseverance, perseverance produces character, and character produces hope."

Tim Keller has made these observations about suffering: "Although nobody wants to suffer, nor do they choose suffering to gain positive outcomes, there are many known benefits that come to those who suffer. They become more resilient, they often gain deeper relationships with those that suffer with them, and they often are prompted to change their priorities and philosophies of life to more-grounded and long-lasting values. Suffering transforms our attitude toward ourselves. It humbles us and removes unrealistic self-regard and pride. Suffering also leads us to examine ourselves and see weaknesses, because it often brings out the worst in us."

C.S. Lewis has said that "in prosperity God whispers to us but in adversity he shouts to us." "When times are good, how do you know if you love God or just love the things that He is giving you or doing for you?" "Finally, suffering is a prerequisite if we are going to help other people who are going through their own trials. Before, we saw others in grief and may have secretly wondered, why can't they just suck it up and go on. Then it comes to us—and ever after, we understand."

The idea that suffering often leaves favorable results is so true that, although we don't often think about it this way, most of us pursue suffering in one form or another. Some people choose to suffer by watching scary movies because they like how they feel when the horror ends. Others prefer running marathons, eating spicy foods, listening to sad songs, climbing steep mountains, or paying people to put them through extreme physical workouts. We have incorporated activities into our lives where the effort and struggle of difficult things serve to provide a greater appreciation for the good things or provide personal satisfaction. At a more extreme level, people will knowingly put themselves in harm's way by enlisting in the military, becoming police or fire personnel, or do other dangerous jobs, not necessarily to suffer, but to experience the challenge, risk or fear, and to attempt to struggle through adverse circumstances. As mentioned earlier, people who embrace suffering and survive are often those who report that they feel a greater sense of meaning and purpose in their lives. Many of the people I know that end up the happiest are not just the ones that have avoided trials, but instead those that have met large challenges in their lives and been able to persevere.

You may have heard of a psychiatrist and Jewish Holocaust survivor named Viktor Frankl who was highly recognized during the 1960s. While in the concentration camps at Auschwitz and Dachau, Frankl observed fellow prisoners and wrote about the attributes that allowed some to maintain a positive attitude while others could not handle the grief and suffering of the terrible circumstances and often ended their own lives. Frankl concluded that the difference between the two groups, and their ability to overcome suffering, was having something in their lives that provided meaning. Those prisoners that could focus their minds on a greater purpose that often included a goal, project or relationship, had something to live for. He wrote, "Those who have a 'why' to live, can bear with almost any 'how'."

My quest for how to deal with suffering and grief after losing my son has led me to many of the same conclusions as Frankl. As I've searched for ways that I might figure out how God could be a good God but still allow such a terrible thing to happen in my life, I created a flow chart that I have included in this book. In my flow chart I examine two directions that most people follow as they try to reconcile the death of a loved one with whether or not God owes them an answer or will ever answer the question of why they have suffered such a great loss.

Grief Flow Chart - *Included at the end of this chapter is a tool developed through my journey called the Grief Flow Chart. The following paragraphs will help to explain the progression through the spiritual search process God took me through as I looked for answers to new "life" questions. The chart reads from top to bottom. Feel free to flip back and forth to the chart for clarity.*

As I explained in Chapter 3, when it comes to asking the "Why God?" question, generally people take one of two approaches in evaluating their thoughts about God, either politely asking or demanding a divine answer to explain their pain. Regardless of their initial attitude, both approaches receive an answer from God that feels more like resounding silence and is often described as a "non-answer." The details of this non-answer have been chronicled in the oldest book of the Bible, Job. In the story of Job, while speaking directly to God and demanding an answer to the "Why did you bring this suffering" question, God verbally responds to Job's inquiry with the response, "Where were you when I laid the earth's foundation?" Job 38:4

In describing his own experience with these same events, C. S. Lewis describes it this way: "When I lay these questions before God, I get no answer. But rather a special sort of 'No' answer. It is not a locked door. It is more like a silent, certainly not uncompassionate, gaze. As though He shook His head not in refusal but waiving the question. Like, 'Peace, child; you don't understand.'"

In my flow chart, for both groups of people upon receiving no obvious answer, some take the path to the left, which is to say, "Okay, God, if you don't give me a satisfactory answer on how you could let this awful thing happen, you must not really exist." Curiously, for the many people who respond this way, I often wonder if God were to have given them an answer aloud in an audible voice like He did to Job, what could He possibly say that they would consider a satisfactory response? I reflect on this not out of judgment, but because I know that had God audibly answered me nearer to the time of my son's death, I honestly can't think of even one thing God could have told me that wouldn't have caused me to want to argue or that I wouldn't have taken exception to! Unfortunately, for these people, and maybe you're one, the next dilemma quickly becomes what are your options from here? Are you really prepared to go the rest of your life with absolutely no belief that there is a God? Tim Keller describes choosing this path this way, "Many try to keep a stiff upper lip and say defiantly, 'I won't let this defeat me!' That is a self-absorbed and self-sufficient response, acting as if you have the strength you need when it will be found only in God. It is unrealistic and even dangerous. Suffering creates inner sorrow; it does make you weak. To deny your hurt—to tell yourself you're just fine, means you will likely pay the price later. You may find yourself blowing up, or breaking down, or falling apart suddenly. Then you will realize you were kidding yourself. You hurt more than you thought you did." As closed-ended and limiting as taking this path can seem, there is still some good news. If you begin to feel that you've made an unwise choice, it is possible to re-trace your steps and go down the other road! For those, like me, who are grieving and questioning, but not yet ready to give up on God, the remainder of the chart outlines the path to the right with the questions and answers that create the logical progression of decisions and conclusions that come as you pursue the next steps after your painful loss.

During my grief journey, I determined that if I couldn't find a way to take a next step toward healing, often the problem was that what I thought I knew was getting in the way of what I needed to discover about God and His ways. In my reading, I came across the Bible verse in Acts 17:24-25 that says, "God made the world ... and he is not served by human hands." Prior to this, I hadn't reflected on the fact that no matter what I, or any of the other 7 billion plus people on the earth thought, God was still going to be the God of this world. From there the logical conclusion is that God doesn't need me, or anyone, or anything, yet we're told over and over that He loves us! Based on that, He must have created me, not for what I could do for Him, but, ultimately, just so that He could love me. As I thought about how that made sense, I was reminded of the reason people have their own children. Most people would say they don't have children so they can be served by them, which is good because it becomes quickly apparent to parents during the early years with children that they're a lot of work! Instead, parents have children initially so that they can love them, even though that isn't how things always turn out for some parents.

This reminds me of the song by George Strait, "Love Without End, Amen":

"I dreamed I died and stood outside the pearly gates … if they know half the things I've done they'll never let me in, then somewhere from the other side I heard these words again. Let me tell you a secret about a father's love. A secret that my daddy said was just between us. He said daddies don't just love their children ever now and then, it's a love without end, Amen."

As I continued thinking my way through the steps of the grieving process on my progression flow chart, I came to another interesting realization. If God doesn't need me, yet He loves me, then the purpose of my life, besides just being loved by Him, must also include my getting the chance to return His love by my thoughts and actions. Again, not because God requires it of me or needs me to, but because I'm his child and it's a way for me to express my appreciation. As I pondered this concept, I realized that my specific objective for the rest of my life also fell along this line of reasoning which becomes the concept of glorifying God.

C.S. Lewis says it this way: "We were not made primarily that we may love God (though we were made for that, too) but that God may love us, that we may become objects in which the Divine love may rest 'well pleased.'"

Before finishing that thought, and lest you might be thinking this seems to be getting too warm and fuzzy, my path from here quickly took a bumpy detour as I realized that because of the recent tragedy in my life, I needed first to convince myself that I trusted God enough to "love him back" at all, since I was still harboring thoughts that he should have intervened and saved my son from dying. This idea reminded me of something I had read by Tim Keller where he said that possibly the reason that God never tells us the whole story of our lives, even when we "demand" the information, is that God wants us to trust and rely on Him solely for who He is and not just what He can do for us. "But it may be that we don't fully love God just for his own sake and that we are subject to the ups and downs depending on how things go in our lives. We do not find our hearts fully satisfied with God unless other things are also going well, and therefore we are without sufficient roots. We must feel that to obey God will bring us no benefits at all. It is at that point that seeking and praying to, and obeying God begins to change us. It's doubtful that this level of reliance in the grace of God can ever be gotten any other way. We may never see the big picture, but only see God." All of this caused me to conclude that since God doesn't rely on us to make him God, it's not hard to imagine that hollow devotion isn't acceptable if it's purely conditional and made with the mandate of a positive outcome.

Once you can accept that tough truth, there really aren't many directions to go besides committing yourself to figuring out what you should and shouldn't expect from God. What has He really promised versus what we may currently believe to be His responsibility in our lives? The next box in the flow chart describes that God has told us that His big promise is that He will give us eternal life in heaven if we believe in Him. That promise, although ultimately fantastic, unfortunately doesn't always seem to help us with our near-term pain. Fortunately, His other commitment is to walk with us through all tough times in our lives on the earth, which probably include right now! Surprisingly, and contrary to what most of us might have thought, God never makes the promise of good health, wealth, or comfort for us or our loved ones. To be clear, it doesn't say we won't have those things, it just gives no earthly guarantees, regardless of our behavior!

The next resolution box in the process of the flow chart acknowledges that grieving has real value. When we're trying to "fix" ourselves because we're suffering, it's easy to rush past taking the time we need to wring out our hearts to God and tell him how we feel. A possible reason we can even try to hurry past this step can even be caused by what seem like proper motives, being not wanting to question God's sovereignty over our lives. The great news is that we don't need to hold back on being honest about our doubts, because based on His track record, He can handle even the bad stuff! What's even better is that while unloading all our heavy baggage on God, we often realize that God actually saw those painful and sad events exactly the way we saw them as if from our own eyes, and that He totally understands!

Once our emotions calm down and we feel the need to move forward, we can often realize that the understanding we've gained about who God is and about our remaining purpose on this earth will lead us to the realization that the suffering we've felt is what allows us to honor God by helping others with their pain. This isn't to say that we won't revisit the grief of loss in our own lives, but only that we will have discovered the sense of meaning and hope that Jewish Holocaust survivor Viktor Frankl talked about that allowed people to survive in the most awful circumstances imaginable.

The grief flow chart journey concludes with these concepts: If our only purpose were to be saved by God and get to heaven, He would have taken us home immediately the moment we put our faith in Him. In the same way, if our only purpose in life was to be the parents, spouses, or friends to those we've lost, He would have also taken us when he took them! But since we're still here, our painful loss can serve to focus us on fulfilling a greater purpose on this earth. The conclusion of my search and of this chart is that the secret to life after loss isn't understanding the "why" of our loss at all, but instead it is for us to truly, and more genuinely, know God! As a final admonition I would implore you to fulfill your new purpose and to pray as I try to each day, "Lord, thanks for loving me. How can I honor you today?"

Romans 5: 1-5 "Therefore, since we are justified by faith, we have peace with God through our Lord Jesus Christ, through whom we have obtained access to his grace in which we stand; and we boast in our hope of sharing the glory of God. And now not only that, but we boast in our sufferings, knowing that suffering produces endurance, and endurance produces character, and character produces hope, and hope does not disappoint us, because God's love has been poured into our hearts through the Holy Spirit that has been given to us." (New Revised Standard)

In Times of Loss...Even Christians Are Still Prone to Ask the "Why?" Question

The reason we struggle may be what we know (or think we know) about God.....

It Seems That God Owes Me Some Kind of Answer
"Let the almighty answer me" - Job 31:35

If I Don't Get A Suitable Answer,
God Must Not Care Or Even Be Real

I'll Still Love You God, But I Feel I Need Some Answer
Psalm 20:9 *"May the King answer us in the day we call."*

Initially, God's "Non- Answer" May Be: Job 38:4 *"Where were you when I laid the foundation of the earth...?"*

OK God, No Good Answer, I'm Out!

BTW....If God Were To Verbally Speak To You About Your Loss, What Reason Today Could He Give That Would Heal You?

I Still Believe, So What Do I Know About God And Why Won't He Answer Me? Job 13:18 Job "Sues" God: *"Behold I have prepared my case; I know I will be vindicated."*

I Will Search The Bible And Other Resources About God For Answers

Now What???

For Instance, in Job 42:5 Job says *"I have heard of you, but now my eyes see you, therefore I retract and repent"* God Never Explains Himself, Yet Job Still Retracts....Why?

I'm Not Giving Up, But Healing Is Coming Slowly, So Maybe I Need To Re-examine My Purpose In This Life?

God Created Everything And Needs Nothing, Yet, Even When I Question Him He Loves Me. Why?
Acts 17:24-25 *"God made the world....and he is not served by human hands"*

Was One Reason God Created Me Just So That He Could Love Me?!! Analogy: Why Do People Have Children?

If My Purpose Is To Be Loved By God and To Glorify Him With My Actions, Based On My Loss, Can I Still Return That Love For God When I Think He Should Have Intervened For Me? Can I Ever Learn To Really TRUST Him Again?

Is The Reason "All Things (Can) Work Together For Good" Romans 8:28, And Why God Never Tells Me The Whole Story Of My Life, Because He Wants Me To TRUST And Rely On Him, As Opposed To Thinking Just What He Can Do Me?

So, Based On His Word, What Can I Expect From God? What Has and Hasn't He Really Promised Me? He Has Promised Eternal Life In Heaven And His Loving Presence Now. Surprisingly, He Hasn't Promised Health, or Wealth, or Comfort!

Grieving Has Great Value, But As We Can Begin To Harness Our Emotions And Move Forward, Understanding God's Promises Will Help Us Learn To Take Our Minds Off Of Ourselves And To Focus On What God Still Has For Us In This Life And To Pursue Our Remaining Purpose.

If Our Purpose On Earth Was Only To Be Saved By God And Go To Heaven, He Would Have Taken Us Home At The Point Of Our Salvation Experience. In The Same Way, If Our Only Purpose Was To Be Parents Or Spouses To Those We've Lost, He Would Have Taken Us Home With Them! While We're Here, We Still Have A Purpose!

Conclusion: The Secret To Life After Loss isn't Knowing "Why", But Truly Knowing God! Fulfill Your Purpose Each Day By Saying "Lord, Thanks For Loving Me, How Can I Love and Glorify You Today?!"

Darren Frame 2019

9

————— ✿ —————

BLAME IT ON GOD!

When someone unexpectedly passes away, it's often human nature for those close to that person to immediately question whether someone or something is to blamed for the tragedy. This quest can often include a lawsuit or the pursuit of another method of punishment for what happened. Sometimes identifying the blame is justified, like when the death is caused by a negligent behavior, like a drunk driver. In other situations, assigning blame can become more questionable, like attempting to blame a doctor or hospital for not saving the person. Certainly, those of us who have lost children can fill in the details that led to their passing. In my case, there were a few occurrences where, had doctors pursued a different strategy, my son might still be alive. However, in my case, there were not any instances where the health care professionals showed mismanagement of my son's case, so assigning blame to them wasn't obvious. Since I didn't have any earthly person whom I felt I could blame, that left me mostly with just

God to question about why my son didn't survive. Since I reasoned that God is all-powerful, it seemed to me that He could have changed the circumstances or any of the other variables, such as decisions on care that would have saved my son, so, in my mind I could only wonder if God were responsible.

Interestingly, it seems that having someone to blame will help alleviate our pain or possibly shift guilt away from ourselves, if that exists. I heard an interview recently with a person that had just come from a trial where someone was found guilty of the death of a person in their family. When asked about the verdict, that person said they could finally rest easy knowing that person was held accountable. While there is certainly value in achieving appropriate justice if a crime has been committed, I sincerely wonder if finding someone guilty in court will provide true relief from a loved one's death?

After considering the alternatives, I'm convinced God is the best choice for placing blame for unexplained tragedies, and, in fact, I would encourage it! Even in those unthinkable situations where you are the one accidentally responsible for someone's death, if you haven't already, I recommend placing the responsibility squarely on God and I think it just may be the most preferable!

Lest you think that I've lost my mind in suggesting something so absurd, let me explain. In all my research about who God is and what He's about, what I can see is that God is the only one capable of properly shouldering blame of this nature. Afterall, who has bigger shoulders than God?

As further explanation, it seems that blaming God has several unique advantages. First, by indicting God for a tragedy, you are first acknowledging that you believe there is a God and that He has enough dominion over life's events that He could have stopped this painful thing from happening. Tim Keller describes it this way: "What's the difference between questioning God and rebelling against God? When we complain about our pain, but we complain to God. When we doubt but doubt to God. When we scream and yell but do it in God's presence. No matter how angry we are but if we continue to address God and to seek God in our worst days, if we do so in a way that we don't allow ourselves to be driven away from God but toward him, God will honor that by upholding us."

Second, by blaming God, you are prompted to ask further the obligatory, related questions, like the one we've discussed in this book, "How could a good God cause or allow something like this to happen?"

Third, if you've considered this question as we've done here, you'll be pleased to find out that God has given us many of the answers to our questions if we're willing to pursue Him for those responses. Consequently, finding God and His ways will be the logical byproduct of this inquiry, which will hopefully provide you with real truth about what's important in your life as well!

Lastly, and the best part of blaming God, is that it's a guarantee there will be more satisfaction and ultimately eternal value with pursuing Him for answers, than if you'd kicked Him to the curb and blamed someone or something else, which could never lead to any real satisfaction or long-term benefit. Tim Keller explains what this looks like if you play the whole thing through: "With Christians we must develop a faith in God himself, not in some agenda we want God to promote. Some people would say 'if we want God to bless us, we must first believe that God will bless us. We must claim our blessing with full assurance that we will get it.' The problem is, we don't see this attitude in the Bible. Often biblical figures did not get the answer they sought and/or like Shadrach, Meshach, and Abednego in Daniel (3:14-15), they said, 'God will deliver us, but even if he doesn't, we will still believe in him and will not waiver.'"

So, what are those answers we might find by pursuing God and how can they help us? To be clear, when I talk about help, I don't mean help like to make the whole painful experience completely go away, at least not in this lifetime. But if you're honest, or even if you have a vivid imagination, what could ever possibly do that anyway? Instead, I mean help like helping to start to fill in that massive hole running through you that leaves you feeling empty and confused. I also mean help like, allowing you to get up from the fetal position or prostrate on the floor, and to face today, tomorrow, and the next day because you've started to put those scattered parts of your life back together. This is the kind of help that the person who has discarded God won't ever know, because they will have trouble ever shaking the hate, spite, or guilt, that they remain under by chronically avoiding the issue.

In summary, even when you start out by blaming God for all that has happened, He can ultimately redeem you and give you the hope for a positive future, no matter how bad things may seem at this moment!

"In the eye of the storm you remain in control, the middle of the war you guard my soul. You alone are the anchor when my sails are torn, your love surrounds me, in the eye of the storm." "When my hopes and dreams are far from me and I'm running out of faith, and I see the future that I pictured slowly fade away. When the tears of pain and heartache are pouring down my face, I find my peace in Jesus' name."

*"And when sickness takes my child away and there's nothing I can do, my only hope is to trust in you." *Eye of the Storm – Ryan Stevenson*

10

———— ❦ ————

PRAYER – WHY DIDN'T IT WORK?

P rayer may be one of the toughest dilemmas to explain if you
prayed to God for the healing of your loved one and still lost him
or her in the process. Especially in times of tragedy, praying ultimately
seems like our only lifeline of hope as we petition God for a positive
result. Because of this, prayer can potentially be viewed as a source
of tremendous disappointment and confusion if the outcome we've
sincerely and genuinely appealed to God for hasn't been realized. In
our daily lives, unanswered or inconclusive prayers can most always be
explained away as misdirected or misunderstood with trite responses
like, "I just needed to be more patient," or "it just wasn't God's plan
for this to happen." This is echoed in the Garth Brooks hit song,
"Thank God for Unanswered Prayers" as he remembers a high school
sweetheart that he thought he wanted to marry, but didn't, ultimately,
to his benefit. However, in times when someone close to us dies, the

finality of death adds a whole different dimension to the perplexing mystery of what godly prayer actually is or isn't.

When it comes to prayer, I have found that managing expectations for ourselves and for others is important but it can also be a very two-edged sword. If we believe God can fulfill our most sincere requests but doesn't, we are prone to ask, "Why not?" or "Why put me through such heartache?" If we try to reduce our expectations to avoid being hopelessly disappointed by what could be a bad outcome, we can feel as though we're selling ourselves short on real faith. Interestingly, with prayer, even positive outcomes can be confusing when they're inconsistent from one prayer to the next. As we mature in our faith, we often come to realize that God wants us to love Him and pray to Him for who He is, and not for what He can do for us, which can be conflicting as we still feel obligated to pray out our feelings and our desires with God. So, how do we sort this all out?

C.S. Lewis said this about the efficacy of prayer:

"Some things are proved by the unbroken uniformity of our experiences. The law of gravitation is established by the fact that, in our experience, all the bodies without exception obey it. Now even if all the things that people prayed for happened, which they do not, this would not prove what Christians mean by the efficacy of prayer. For prayer is a request. The essence of the request, as distinct from compulsion, is that it may or may not be granted. And if an infinitely wise Being listens to the requests of finite and foolish creatures, of course He will sometimes grant and sometimes refuse them. Invariable 'success' in prayer would not prove the Christian doctrine at all. It would prove something much more like magic – a power in certain human beings to control, compel, the course of nature. There are, no doubt, passages in the New Testament which may seem at first to promise an invariable granting of our prayers. But that cannot be what they mean. For in the very heart of the story we meet a glaring instance to the contrary. In Gethsemane the holiest of all petitioners (Jesus) prayed three times that a certain cup might pass from Him. It did not. After that the idea that prayer is recommended to us as a sort of infallible gimmick may be dismissed."

As I've tried to examine this issue in my own life, I started with the question, "Why does God want us to pray?" In the Bible we are commanded to pray, so it must be important to God that we abide. What I discovered was that prayer is never encouraged just so that God can find out what we need, because Jesus has already told us "Your father in heaven knows what you need before you ask him," Matt. 6:8. So, there must be some other reason. To do a more thorough study of what these reasons might be, I spent a lot of time in Wayne Grudem's book, "Bible Doctrine", which takes all the verses from the Bible and groups them topically. Fortunately, it wasn't hard to locate the answer to my question about what prayer really is and why we should pursue it. Grudem explains that God seemingly wants us to pray so our trust in Him will increase. Secondly, He also wants us to love Him and have fellowship by having conversations with Him. The third reason God wants us to pray is so we, as his creatures, are involved in activities that are eternally important. We pray so the work of the kingdom is advanced. The fourth reason is that in praying we give glory to God. Praying in humble dependence on God indicates that we are genuinely convicted of His wisdom, love, goodness, and power.

As you can see by these more technical explanations of prayer, while they may not initially get to the heart of your concerns, the glaring item that's apparent is that none of the reasons for praying actually includes any guarantees that asking God for our desires, no matter how legitimate, will lead to outcomes that will meet our plans or preferences. This truth still left me feeling empty since I didn't see how God could not want to comply with my requests if they were genuine and made good sense to me. So, I continued to look into prayer at a deeper level. I thought to myself, maybe I'm doing the prayer thing all wrong and not praying in the right way.

My first thought was that I could be sending my prayers to the wrong person in the Trinity, which includes the Father, Son, and Holy

Spirit. Who should we pray to? Since we're told that the God of the Bible manifests himself as three distinct persons, but is only one God, maybe I needed a different approach. Bible Doctrine answers that question in this way: In the Bible there is a clear pattern of praying directly to God the Father, but there are other indications that prayer spoken directly to Jesus is appropriate. Even prayers to the Holy Spirit are not forbidden, although not common in the Bible. So, there seems to be no specifically wrong technique there.

The next idea I had was to ask, "How should we pray?" Do we pray for what we want or let God decide what's right by only praying for the fulfillment of God's will related to any issue? It turns out that this has been a question that has perplexed people for thousands of years. C. S. Lewis wrote this in his "Scraps", God in the Dock: "Praying for particular things", said I, "always seems to me like advising God how to run the world. Wouldn't it be wiser to assume he knows best?" "On the same principle," said he, "I suppose you never ask a man next to you to pass the salt, because God knows best whether you ought to have salt or not. And I suppose you never take an umbrella, because God knows best whether you ought to be wet or dry." "That's quite different," I protested. "I don't see why," said he. "The odd thing is that He should let us influence the course of events at all. But since He lets us do it in one way, I don't see why He shouldn't let us do it in the other."

The Bible Doctrine answer for the question of how to pray and what to pray for reveals this: Pray according to God's will. "This is the confidence which we have in him, that if we ask anything according to his will, he hears us." 1 John 5:14 But how do you know what God's will is? The first way to know God's will is if something we are asking for lines up with God's will as stated in the Bible. But there are certainly lots of times we don't know what God's will is because it is not mentioned in scripture. In those cases, we often must admit that we simply don't know what God's will is. In such cases, we should ask him for deeper understanding and then pray for what seems best to us, giving reasons to the Lord why, in our best understanding of the situation, what we are praying for seems best … and follow it up with "If it is your will."

This explanation touches on the question about how much we can know about our circumstances and what only God knows. For instance, in the Bible, God told Abraham to sacrifice his son, Isaac on an altar as a tribute to God. God first commanded Abraham to sacrifice his son, and even allowed Abraham to have his son tied down with the knife in his hand before God told Abraham to stop and not kill his son. Since God knew, He wasn't going to allow the killing, why did He insist that the whole situation play out before telling Abraham to stop? What seems to be clear is that God felt it was necessary for Abraham himself to know that he would not falter, but would directly follow God's command. According to this line of reasoning, some parts of prayer assume our ability to have free will, while still allowing God to have the ability to control the situation ultimately as He teaches us through our own actions. C. S. Lewis describes the perplexing topic this way: "The imagination will, no doubt try to play tricks on us at this point. I will ask, 'Then if I stop praying can God go back and alter what has already happened?' No. The event has already happened and one of its causes has been the fact that you are asking such questions instead of praying. It will ask, 'Then if I begin to pray can God go back and alter what has already happened?' No. The event has already happened and one of its causes was your present prayer. Thus, something does really depend on my choice. My free act contributes to the cosmic shape. That contribution is made in eternity or 'before all worlds'; but my consciousness of contributing reaches me at a particular point in the time-series."

Regardless of our ability to understand different nuances of prayer, confusion about the efficacy, meaning the successes and failures of prayer, can still easily become a difficult and crushing issue for us when the answers to certain prayers seem so inconsistent. For me, the complaint went something like this: "I, and many other people, prayed for my son to be healed and he still died. How can we say that prayer is effective and why would we continue wasting our time? And, furthermore, going forward how can we even think about praying for insignificant small details, when God didn't even answer the big prayers that included the difference between life and death?"

If you've vocalized these questions to God or others or thought them to yourself, you're not alone. My wife and I come from Christian homes and counting our friends, our parents, our parents' friends, and including several networks of prayer groups, etc., I'm quite convinced at about 5,000 people likely prayed for my son Jared to survive his illness over the course of several days he was in the hospital. If God's plan for Jared's life could have been influenced by numbers of people praying or by direct and specific prayers, the fact that we didn't receive a positive outcome certainly wasn't for lack of trying!

As in my case, the most difficult part of understanding prayer is to reconcile the dilemma of "What about unanswered prayers?" Bible Doctrine says we must recognize that as long as God is God and we are his creatures, there will always seem to be unanswered prayers. This is because God keeps hidden His own wise plans for the future, and even though people pray, many events will not come about until the time God has decreed. We must keep remembering that He will give us the strength sufficient for each day (Deut 33:25) and sometimes prayers will go unanswered in this life.

In trying to create for myself a healthy outlook on what prayer is and what it isn't, I've found that insight from some Jewish rabbis, like Steve Leder can be helpful. In his book "More Beautiful than Before," Leder has a perspective that, as a Christian, I was a bit surprised to find extremely helpful. I often appreciate that practicing Jews are very honest about their view of God because they don't try to make God into something that He's not. This perspective is likely because the God that is presented in the Old Testament of the Bible seems willing to advance the concept of hard truth in many circumstances. Leder says, "I don't think praying to God prevents disasters or cures cancer, because I don't think God causes disasters or gives people cancer in the first place." There can certainly be debate concerning where bad things come from and whether God causes them or allows them, but if God is all-powerful, all-knowing, and in-control, at the very least, it makes sense that our hardships are not a surprise to Him. If God doesn't see our circumstances as unexpected, like Abraham with Isaac, His plan must include the events in our lives and would also include the provision that He will give us the strength necessary to persevere through our most difficult times.

My other reason for appreciating the perspective of Jews like Steve Leder, is because it stands to reason that they aren't jaded by some of the modern Christian teaching that portrays Jesus' love for us only as a responsive love designed to cater to our desires rather than a love with biblical guidelines originating with God's plans for the world and not just our own. Just because Jesus says He has unconditional love for us obviously doesn't mean that He has obligated Himself to fix every problem and hardship we have on this earth. In other words, God either causes or allows bad things to happen to good people for reasons that are beyond our understanding. As an example, as parents, we love our children, but that doesn't mean we always run ahead of them and to make sure there will be no trials or difficult problems in their lives. Often, it is our obligation as good parents to let them work through certain hardships that will allow them to learn valuable lessons. From a practical standpoint, we therefore know this works for us as adults as well. However, I must admit that the lessons I've learned from losing my son are the most difficult and expensive lessons that I could ever have imagined learning, and I would be happy to forfeit that knowledge in a minute if I could. However, I can say that although I don't have the eternal perspective that God has, just having been down the road a little ways from losing my son, I can certainly say that my faith in God has unquestionably been strengthened and have a very unique sense that there will be coming a time when God will allow me to recognize all the good that has come from my tragedy.

If you're like me, as you try to extinguish the fireball of grief you might be currently dealing with, the questions likely at the top of your mind are, 1) how to pray, 2) what to pray for, and 3) what your prayers mean to God and to you. My view on prayer, as with many of my perspectives on the character of God, has been painfully forced to change from what I thought I knew prior to my son's death. Like many people, my previous prayers were mostly comprised of requests of God, maybe a few praises, and some brief thankyou's from when really good things happened in my life. I feel fortunate that that I've felt and seen specific prayers in my life answered directly by God in the past as best I can tell. However, with Jared's passing, I've been forced to try to reconcile why the biggest and most important request of my life, that seemed completely genuine, logical, and legitimate, did not result in a positive outcome that included my son being saved from his illness. Since Jared has passed, I have changed my approach for praying based on what I've learned from reading people's perspectives like those of Steve Leder and others. My emphasis now includes an attempt to surrender to God's will for my life prior to talking with God as well as trying to be committed to the idea that He knows what is best for my life and all this regardless of my current circumstances or desires. From there, my prayer dialogue with God has changed to asking Him to support me with wisdom, patience, and love as I react to the outcomes in my life, and not necessarily just to protect me from unwanted circumstances. I now also try to pray specifically for strength for myself and my family as we encounter the disappointments that occur in our lives. Conversely, I try to resist praying "for" something to happen, but instead, asking to be "released" from focusing on the things that inhibit a closer walk with God through those trials, like from fear, anger, and doubt. Also, I pray for God to assist me in changing my perceptions and attitude, as opposed to asking God to change His plan for my life. By looking at prayer this way, I find it helps to divorce my expectations for certain results in individual events, of which unwanted outcomes can make me question God's wisdom when things don't go as I had planned.

The best way to demonstrate this changed philosophy is to again use the analogy of being parents to our children. If a child makes a request of the parent, it's the parents' prerogative to choose some response that involves acting on, or not acting on, the request. Sometimes the request is acknowledged and granted, sometimes the child is told why the request will not being granted, and sometimes there is no immediate response for a reason that may be only possibly known by the parent. In any instance, the parents' actions don't come because they didn't hear what the child said. Additionally, just as parents generally want to keep the lines of communication open with their children, the Bible makes clear that God wants to hear from us. He wants us to take time to talk with him and meditate on our relationship with him and share our lives with him through prayer. The more genuine and transparent our communication is with God, it stands to reason that He would appreciate it, not at all unlike we as parents love to hear our children tell us about their lives, feelings, fears, and victories. Of course, as parents we have reasons we don't always immediately act on the requests of our children, and we certainly don't always grant them everything they ask for immediately when they ask it. Our wisdom leads us to know that some things that children want aren't good for them in the moment and some things won't serve them well later either. Although this analogy breaks down at this point because we can't view ourselves as being all-knowing like God, we do understand how events are likely to play out in our children's lives from previous experiences of our own. Our answers to requests from our children can be yes, no, sometimes later, and occasionally never. Also, our answers are not always predicated on things that seem urgent to our children or even as well-meaning requests. Sound familiar? Also, it's interesting that, as parents, sometimes we say 'yes' and even grant our children's requests, knowing that trouble is likely ahead. We sometimes will take this course of action knowing that we want the children to learn from the consequences of their actions.

You may be thinking, yes, I understand the analogy but how could a request to save someone's life ever be a bad thing or a request God wouldn't honor? While this is certainly a legitimate question, and one that no one on the earth can answer, if you genuinely believe in the sovereign nature and wisdom of God to know all about the past, the present, and the future, at some point you must resign yourself to admit that God must have a reason that you can't see or understand. I like to think that the apparent inconsistency in God's character that occurs when He doesn't affirmatively answer our most obvious and seemingly logical requests points to the fact that, while our time on the earth is important, our lives in God's eternal view might appear different to Him than they do to us. Phillip Yancy says this, "When yearning for a miraculous resolution to a problem, do we make our loyalty to God contingent on whether he reveals himself yet again in the seen world? In his mercy, God may answer a prayer of mixed motives – witness all the 'Lord, if you only get me out of here …' foxhole conversions. But that is for him to decide, not us."

Importantly, we must remember that God has not promised us or our children a healthy, trouble-free life, nor one that doesn't include suffering. The life led by Jesus, the apostles, and most every other influential person tracked in the Bible, certainly makes that truth plainly clear. Both the Old Testament and New Testament are filled with stories about difficult events encountered by many of God's people. However, the promise God has given us is that He won't leave us alone as we navigate through life's rough waters. In other words, your prayers, if properly framed, should involve taking God up on his promise to bring you through your suffering, and not just necessarily to eliminate it. The bottom line is, if we continue to lean on God in the toughest of times, throwing all our pain and sorrow his way through our prayers, I believe He will not refuse to answer our prayers in just the way we have prayed them.

As an additional note, after my son Jared's passing, I really struggled when I listened to other people praying and asking God for what I considered the small and temporal things in life. I couldn't help but feel that if God didn't answer my huge request to spare my son's life, how could He possibly care about someone's sore back, or a safe trip, or a friend that had just lost their job! Even today, I must continue to remind myself that God is our Father, and he does want to hear even the small concerns in our lives along with the bigger things, all as part of having the open line of communication that we talked about earlier. I also must remember that just because God's wisdom doesn't always align with my preferences (just as our children don't like it when parents don't act on requests immediately), if those things we bring to Him in prayer are part of His will for our lives, no matter how small, they may still be given to us for reasons we'll never know.

Last, if you've suffered loss and your prayer request is for God to heal your heart, I believe from my own experience, that you're putting yourself on the track toward recovery from the deep pain you may be feeling. I can also tell you as an observer of others that have suffered tragic losses, those that are Christians are the ones who ultimately gain more comfort from their beliefs than those who are not seeking God. I believe this is because God works inside our souls. From there He walks where we walk, sees through our eyes, and experiences the pain along with us, so that He knows exactly how to help. Undoubtedly, simply having the experience of feeling that you're not alone in your pain and that someone is sharing the grief with you can provide a miraculous sense of comfort. The Bible tells us that the reason Jesus came to earth, suffered, and died on the cross, was so He would know our pain firsthand and be able to comfort us in a way that a distant God could not. I hope this kind of peace will find you because I know that it can provide comfort that can't be found elsewhere. Continue talking with God!

"Who Am I, that the Lord of all the earth, would care to know my name, would care to feel my hurt? Who am I, that the bright and morning star would choose to light the way, for my ever-wondering heart? Not because of who I am, but because of what you've done. Not because of what I've done, but because of who you are. I'm a flower quickly fading,

*here today and gone tomorrow, a wave tossed in the ocean, a vapor in the wind. Still, you hear me when I'm calling, Lord, you catch me when I'm falling, and you've told me who I am, I am yours!" *Who Am I – Casting Crowns*

11

------ ❦ ------

EVEN IF GOD TOLD YOU "WHY", WOULD IT REALLY HELP?

T he difficulty in writing a book that asks questions, like "Why God will allow bad things to happen," is that attempting to discuss potential answers can quickly get into deep water intellectually and theologically. What's even worse is that the answer to the "Why now, God?" question leads to the even more perplexing question of "How could a good God allow bad, evil, unfortunate, and even catastrophic things to happen, ever?" Much of the methodology for answering these questions centers on the concept that God's economy is not necessarily our economy. While this is true, the next question that comes up is if our view is so different than God's, does anything makes sense? C. S. Lewis addresses the question this way: "On the one hand, if God's moral judgement differs from ours so that our "black" may be His "white," we can mean nothing by calling Him good; for to say, "God is good," while asserting that His goodness is wholly other than ours, is really to say, "God is we know not what." "The Divine 'goodness' differs from ours, but is not sheerly different; it differs from ours not as white from black but as a perfect circle from a child's first attempt to draw a wheel. But when the child has learned to draw, it will know that the circle it then makes is what it was trying to make at the very beginning."

What's interesting is that even though humans have been forever asking these really important questions, those of us who have experienced loss may have only considered genuinely pursuing the answers because tragedy has caused us to have a specific reason to want to know. Unfortunately, no matter what your reason is for asking God "Why?", even if it comes from the most sincere, honest, and pleading of circumstances, the true answer remains the same. Crickets! God's seeming silence.

If you feel the desire to review the litany of human history regarding the question of why God allows evil and death, Tim Keller's book, "Walking With God through Pain and Suffering," dedicates one-third of its 300 pages to the various theories and it is truly a fascinating study. However, if a summary of the various theories works for you at the moment, then here are the primary answers to the question, which happen to correspond to the ways people view God, as taken from a sermon by Pastor Mark Driscoll while he was going through the book of James:

1. *There is no God, so the there is no why question. – Atheism*
2. *God is not all-powerful and can't stop evil. – Finite Godism*
3. *God is not all-knowing, so doesn't control the existence of evil. – Evolutionary Godism or Open Theism*
4. *God is not all-good, so evil should be expected. – Pantheism or Panentheism*
5. *There is no such thing as suffering and evil. – Subjectivism or Pluralism*

6. *God is not done perfecting the world yet, so, we need to live patiently by faith. - Christianity*

When it comes to the "Why God?" question, if you're like me and it feels like you won't be at peace until you have some sort of answer to just how God could have allowed the death of your child or loved one, I'd like you to consider the following hypothetical circumstance. If Jesus were sitting right next to you now, even in the despair you may be experiencing since your recent loss, would the first words you would say in His presence really include the "Why God" question about your loss? Possibly your initial response is "Of course it would, because I want to know the reason for my loss more than anything in the world."

Well, I've thought about this scenario many times since my son died in 2016, and while, like you, I originally thought I would demand to hear the reason for my son's death, I've since come to a different conclusion. Believe me, I have been to the emotional bottom, too, and I know what it feels like to be completely lost in sorrow and grief. But remember, this is really Jesus aka: God sitting right there! Because of that, likely before you could even speak, He would look deep into your eyes and call you by name, even though you've never seen Him before. Then He would tell you that He's known you all your life and even before you were born. He might tell you about several events from your life and even talk openly about your private thoughts that no one else could even know, including all the times you've cried as you've lamented the loss of your child or loved one. He could describe the actual moment that the person died and could explain the sad event just as you saw it and from your own perspective. I must tell you, I'm not an emotional person, but thoughts like this can bring me to tears.

If I concentrate, and if this were actually Jesus, I believe that everything else in that moment would instantly begin to fade away, and I mean EVERYTHING! Even those recent memories of the worst thing that has likely ever happened to you would even seem secondary in the moment. Personally, as bad as I want to know the "Why?" of my son's passing, I believe my reaction would be to throw my arms around Him and recognize Him as my Savior and thank Him over and over for coming to sit with me in that moment and how I would realize that there was nothing that could have happened that He didn't control. I think, in that moment, the words that would come out of my mouth would be that it was His love that I needed beyond all the things I thought I wanted only minutes before. You may want to pause for a moment and really put yourself into this picture and hope that this is the exact realization you'll have one day.

If even after this word picture you remain unconvinced and you're still certain that your first question for Jesus would be "Why did my loss happen?", fair enough. Here is the information I promised that may provide some answers. However, before reading on, you must remember that this remains one of the most complex questions in the history of the world, and some of the conclusions can be difficult to hear.

The core of the "Why God?" question is the shortened version of the longer question "How could a good God let something terrible like this happen?" Further expanded, that statement goes something like this: "If God is willing and would like to prevent bad and evil things from happening, but doesn't, He must not be all powerful. If He is able, but not willing, then He is not loving. If He is both able and willing, then why do bad things still happen?" You'll notice that this is also the strongest of objections, not just to death, but to the very existence of God, which is why it also serves as the basis for any organized religion, like Christianity.

In answering this question, Tim Keller, in his book, "Walking With God Through Pain and Suffering," first spends several chapters on what different people and societies in history have thought about the concept of suffering. According to Keller, "before suffering is a philosophical issue (about God), it is a practical crisis." The real question may be, "how do I survive this?" Keller says, if we begin the discussion with the traditional problem of the existence of evil eliminating the very existence of God, it would give the impression that only the belief in a traditional God is the worldview that is challenged by the existence of suffering at all. Previously in his book, Keller discusses in-depth that throughout history people have battled suffering, regardless of their belief in God, and how each philosophy has its own challenges.

To further unpack the question, the main requirement is that we must admit that, since the evil and the suffering that lead to death don't make sense to us, then we've consequently decided that the death of our loved one just can't have any redeeming qualities under any circumstance. If you're following this explanation at least this far, hold on tight, because the water gets even deeper. The next question is that if there actually is a God, additional theories about how God operates are necessary. The first question is how does God interact with our free will, and especially, how we can decide to choose evil over good, if God is ultimately in control of everything? The answer to this question also includes how much or how little God has or allows dominion over our choices. C. S. Lewis describes the dilemma like this: If a game is played, it must be possible to lose it. If the happiness of a creature lies in self-surrender, no one can make that surrender but himself and he may refuse. I would pay any price to be able to say truthfully 'All will be saved.' But my reason retorts, 'Without their will or with it?' If I say 'Without their will,' I at once perceive a contradiction; how can the supreme voluntary act of self-surrender be involuntary? If I say, 'With their will,' my reason replies, 'How if they will not give in?'

While these are difficult questions to tackle, even conceptually, acquiring the answers doesn't always help, because they only explain the moral evils that are caused directly by people. They don't help us answer the questions about natural evils like diseases, tornados or accidents. In my case, although human error may have played a small part in my son's death, no one person caused my son's death because he died of an infection. So, now what?

So, what about suffering and why doesn't God eliminate it? Even when God was interacting more directly with people on the earth, as with the prophets in the Old Testament of the Bible, suffering existed.

Jesus suffered. Peter and the apostles mostly all suffered. And Paul, who may have been the greatest strictly human representative for God ever on Earth, suffered and was beheaded for his faith. But the question remains, shouldn't God be helping us to avoid suffering? After all, nobody benefits from suffering. (or do we?) In several places, the Bible makes it clear that in this life, we will all suffer, but even though it is acknowledged by God and has existed since before creation, we still don't want to believe it or accept it. But, since it seems to be a foregone conclusion that we will all suffer, the question becomes, what are we going to do about it? In the letter to the Thessalonians, the apostle Paul talks about all the benefits of suffering, like character, wisdom, and the perseverance that comes from powering our way through. Because of this, the question becomes, "Is there a way we should embrace suffering or even desire it in some way?" Tim Keller describes it this way: God seems to have mapped out a plan for history that allows evil as part of it. That confuses and angers us, but human stories of perseverance, maybe like yours, allow us to pull back the veil for just an instant and show us God will allow evil only to the degree that it brings back the very opposite of what it intends.

I'm sure by now you're wondering if we'll ever get to the point, or maybe you've even forgotten where we were going? After all, this is supposed to be a brief book with some useful answers and not just more questions. To get back on track, here's where this conversation is headed. Regardless of whether you believe in God or not, suffering, pain, and even death exist, although we'd wish otherwise. Therefore, you can choose to say there is no God or convince yourself that God is not in control. But if you divorce God from your reality, you're also saying there is no such thing as a moral standard for good or evil, because, if there is no divine basis for those things, then suffering can only be classified as what you personally determine to be good or bad at any particular time.

In this line of reasoning, anything we believe apart from the existence of God just becomes a set of random ideas with no foundational standard. And, if so, the next question quickly becomes "If there is no God, then who gets to determine which outcomes are acceptable and which aren't?" Does each person independently get to decide what's considered right and wrong on his own? Does the government? How about social media, or maybe just what we call public opinion? If current opinion is the only determinate for what's right, good can be bad one day, and bad can be good another. So, good and bad are subject to changing moment by moment. The application of all this is that, although an atheist can conveniently say he doesn't have to contend with the "Why God?" question because he doesn't believe God exists, by abandoning belief in God, an atheist also must abandon the idea that there is any real help for his pain outside of himself when it comes to the source of suffering. Tim Keller describes the atheist's view like this, "Interestingly, the atheist doesn't have to answer the question of why an all-powerful God allows bad things to happen. An atheist would say that they are free to concentrate on our fate within this world. While atheists think they escape problems, they also fail to address the problem of what is right and what is wrong and ethical standards. "The atheist might say, 'we live to find happiness'. But when suffering makes the conditions for happiness go away, by definition, it also destroys your reason to keep living." So the problem of evil, suffering, and death as it pertains to belief in God, becomes an even larger problem with no belief in God.

What seems worse about a worldview that doesn't include God is what to do if you don't think you already have all the answers, especially when others give conflicting opinions. Which explains why, if left to ourselves, we constantly slide into a type of depression that says, "that's the way it is," or "life is awful, and we don't have any hope of that changing!" That perspective just isn't ultimately appealing to me. Does it appeal to you?

During the early days of the COVID-19 pandemic, many people came to realize for the first time that the entire planet is much more connected and fragile than they thought. For many, the virus demonstrated that there could be events so beyond our control, that we don't really hold the keys to our destiny while here on Earth. With COVID-19, many people were frustrated that they couldn't seem to figure out exactly who was to blame, so the pursuit of blaming someone has continued to be an obsession for lots of people. It has also been interesting to see how many people shifted their faith from themselves to local or federal governments, assuming that those in power could save us from the problem. Of course, this strategy didn't exactly work out either. The fact that COVID-19 may continue to be responsible for many deaths has once again brought some unique questions about how the sovereignty of God really manifests itself in our lives.

The pandemic also brought another question to mind for some: If God were to always tell us His exact reason for taking our loved ones prematurely from COVID-19 or any other cause, could we honestly say that we'd be the least bit satisfied with any "Why God?" answer He could offer? What part of His plan would we possibly be ready to accept? Wouldn't we just demand to have your loved ones back immediately? Here is what C. S. Lewis says about asking God for his wife back after her death from cancer: "Come back, is all for my own sake. I never even raised the question whether such a return, if it were possible, would be good for her. ... Could I have wished for anything worse? Having just got once through death, to come back and then at some later date, have all her dying to do over again?"

It can be perplexing to think that if God were to tell us everything about the death of our loved ones ahead of time, just knowing the future would actually be a miracle in itself. The question is, would that miracle cause you to place or renew your faith in God, and would it make you ready to defer to His ultimate wisdom for the rest of your life? Or, conversely, would you just find yourself wanting to argue with God about His reasons behind the events surrounding your loved one's death or in your life? Wouldn't you still want to accuse him of being unfair?

I love what Phillip Yancy says about why God doesn't step in and make things "fair" for us: "Why the delay? Why does God let evil, and pain so flagrantly exist, even thrive on this planet? Why does he let us do slowly and blunderingly what he could do in an eyeblink? He holds back for our sakes. Re-creation involves us; we are, in fact, at the center of His plan. The wager, the motive of all human history, is to develop us, not God. Our very existence announces to the powers in the universe that restoration is underway. Every act of faith by every one of the people of God is like the tolling of a bell, and like the faith of Job's reverberates through the universe."

In thinking about this heavy subject, you might now admit that upon further reflection, there is probably nothing that God could tell you that would immediately cause you to accept the death of your loved one with any sense of satisfaction. For this reason, Tim Keller and many others have concluded that God will never allow us to see the entirety of our lives all at once because the results would be disastrous. And what's worse, it wouldn't even strengthen our faith. Can you imagine receiving visibility of your whole life's events prior to losing your loved one? That and other occurrences would have us constantly distraught and thinking about changing all our circumstances so as not to lead to any bad events. We'd drive ourselves completely nuts doing nothing but rearranging all our plans, which would also include the plans of others around us, all just to avoid bad things from ever happening. And, what if we ran out of bandwidth to help everyone we wanted to help? That kind of existence would by any measure be a horrible way to live and would almost surely never include any joy.

12

———— ◈ ————

WHERE WAS GOD THROUGH ALL OF THIS? THREE WAYS GOD MAY HAVE ALREADY SHOWED UP

When really bad things happen, an almost involuntary response can be, "Where was God when I needed him in my time of crisis?" The question of where to find God in your painful circumstances is so natural that the apostle Paul even asked this same question. Some don't know that Jesus asked this question, too. We know that Paul asked God not once, but three times, to remove his "thorn in the flesh" (many people think this may have been a vision problem Paul had, but nobody knows for sure). It seems likely that in those three recorded requests Paul openly wondered why God hadn't stepped in and lifted his burden as requested, prompting him to ask again. Even Jesus asked, "Father, why have you forsaken me?" as he died on the cross. Luke 22:4

It is equally common to hear well-meaning people offer the advice that God is always right there with you in your suffering. I can tell you from experience that when you lose a child, it doesn't always feel like God is right there with you. Maybe, more than any time in your life, during these days, it can seem that you're all alone in your grief, which is ironically strange, because there are also undoubtedly people all around you grieving the loss as well.

C. S. Lewis, in "The Problem with Pain", describes looking for God like this." Meanwhile, where is God? When you are happy, so happy that you have no sense of needing Him, so happy you are tempted to feel His claims upon you an interruption, if you remember yourself and turn to Him with gratitude and praise, you will be – or so it feels – welcomed with open arms. But go to Him when your need is desperate, when all other help is in vain, and what do you find? A door double bolted from the inside. After that, silence. You may as well turn away. The longer you wait, the more emphatic the silence will become. There are no lights in the windows. It might be an empty house. Was it ever inhabited? It seemed so once. And that seeming was as strong as this. What can this mean? Why is He so present a commander in our time of prosperity and so very absent a help in our time of trouble?

So, in these times, how can you recognize where God is and what he is doing? The bad news is that it's mostly up to you to do the looking; but, the good news is that it may not be a difficult search if you have the right road map. Below, I have listed three ways that God may have already showed during your time of need, even if you weren't aware of His presence at the time:

1. The first way God often shows up for you is through those people who have come around you during your time of crisis. This may sound cliché; but, if instead of seeing them as your family and friends, you think back on their presence collectively as God showing up with the capacity to help, it makes perfect sense. The beauty of taking this perspective is that this may make it more comfortable to accept help from them and to ask them for things you need, and also not to find

fault with them if they say things that are awkward as they try to console you. Don't overlook the spirit of forgiveness that you may need to extend to others, because, as we've talked about, people don't all handle grief the same way. It's easy for them not to know how to help in just the way you prefer. The beauty is that God is providing his presence to you by working through the people that love you. Sometimes, you just have to attempt to see things with a different perspective.

2. God can be present by giving you a change of attitude about your life. You may not be accustomed to outwardly showing emotion or sharing your heart by confiding in others. You may even have a habit of burying your feelings deep down inside to avoid making yourself vulnerable or beholden to anyone. Regrettably, if you try to convince yourself that you're not hurting that badly right now, the consequences of closing yourself off often can make an already bad situation worse. No matter how wounded, confused, upset or downright angry you might feel, simply acknowledging those frustrations, while openly, and maybe even verbally, praying to God, may result in your feeling that the burden is being lifted almost immediately. I'm not saying that talking to God and genuinely confiding in him (maybe for the first time) will automatically help you stop hurting; but, fighting against God and, consequently, being at war with yourself has absolutely no chance of changing your situation and can't possibly be good for your outlook. Just closing your eyes and simply telling God that you're not going to fight against him may give you an immediate sense that He's right there listening. Clearly, there won't be a flash of lightning, and the relief won't all come at once; but, over time, it's almost guaranteed that the weight will begin to lift, and the enormous hole you feel running right through your heart will slowly begin to close.

3. Lastly, you may see God when you look at others who are hurting. When you reach outside yourself and begin to empathize with others that are going through the same kind of pain that you are, God can show up. When a devastating crisis occurs, like losing a child or a loved one, a curious thing happens with your family and close friends. Each person becomes introspective and begins to focus on how the terrible event is affecting him/her individually and, further, each one personalizes what he/she could have done differently that might have changed the outcome. When my son passed away, my wife grieved very emotionally. My older son internalized the situation by saying it would have been better if this terrible thing had happened to him. Jared's best friend and his girlfriend became lost in certain types of guilt based on their own experiences. Even Jared's grandparents processed the situation by personalizing the tragedy in their own ways. Every person in our extended family was in such agony that it became difficult for most of us to see beyond our own personal hurt in that moment. The message to take from this is that each of the people around you and their individual grief experience can represent an opportunity for you to put your own pain aside for a little while to sit with each one and listen intently. Just having your presence as someone who shares the grief is a very real way for you and others to feel God's presence in the situation.

As with most pain, the acute grief period for me gradually subsided, and when it did, an effective way for me to see God's presence amid the suffering was to force myself to start reaching out to those closest to me. Just the act of consciously going beyond our own specific heartaches and attempting to understand the perspective from another person's viewpoint have incredible healing properties that come directly from God. Certainly, the primary message Jesus had throughout his time on earth was simply to love others. I believe that this message can be expanded to say that God will show up through us and heal us as we perform acts of kindness toward others.

As time goes on, this healing that comes from reaching outside yourself can also be felt by reaching out to people you may not even know, but that are also going through a grief period. Based on my experience, when people observe that you've been able to maintain a Godly perspective while you're weathering the most difficult storm of your life, they will begin to call on you to help others who are in their darkest days as well. While helping others might be the last thing on your mind early in your intense and immediate pain, be aware that one of the ways God may attempt to show up and heal you is for you to reach out to others that are on a similar grief journey. Even just taking the time to tell your story to other people that are suffering will allow you both to realize that you're not the only one living through unspeakably difficult circumstances. During these times, God's presence can be felt in a whole different way.

"'I was hungry, and you gave me food, I was thirsty, and you gave me drink, I was a stranger and you welcomed me, I was naked and you clothed me, I was sick and you visited me, I was in prison and you came to me.' Then the righteous will answer Jesus, saying 'Lord, when did we see you hungry and feed you, or thirsty and give you drink? And when did we see you as a stranger and welcome you, or naked and clothe you?' And when did we see you sick or in prison and visit you?' And the King will answer them, 'Truly I say to you, as you did to one of the least of these my brothers, you did it to me.'" Matthew 25:35-40 English Standard Version

Ray Boltz describes the feeling in his song, "The Anchor Holds": "I've had dreams, … But I never knew, those dreams could slip right through, like they were only grains of sand." "The anchor holds, though the ship is battered, the anchor holds, though the sails are torn, I have fallen on my knees, as I face the raging seas, but the anchor holds, in spite of the storm."

13

GIVE IT TO ME STRAIGHT –
WHAT CAN I EXPECT NOW?

Two words describe what you can expect going forward—waiting and reflecting. While working through the dark times of the grieving process, it may seem strangely like you're waiting for something to happen, although you're not sure what. For me, it took a year or more to feel subconsciously like I wasn't going to wake up from a bad dream and my son would be alive just as before. Additionally, I've heard many people say that they felt like a door would open or they would come around a corner and there would be the person that had died just as if nothing had happened. As time passes, the acute pain begins to subside, and you begin to heal, although you typically don't realize that you're healing since it never seemed like you could heal. Along the way you may hear or read the Bible verse in Romans which is often quoted, "God works all things for good ..." Unfortunately, the detailed information that verse doesn't include is that the fulfillment of working all things for good almost always involves the unwelcomed concept of waiting, and maybe even waiting beyond this life!

I'm not proud of it, and I realize it's probably a sign of immaturity, but, nevertheless, I'm an extremely impatient person. If you are good at waiting, bless you! The waiting process for me is usually painful and even thinking about waiting makes it worse. For me, waiting feels like my skin is going to crawl right off my body if only a few more minutes pass and things don't speed up. Speaking from experience, when it comes to healing, and even having seen God's timing as He actually did work" things for good" in my life, I can still say that it often takes quite a bit longer for good to come than I'd have chosen. I was ready for answers to "Why?" questions now. Here's the thing, in looking back on your life, if every event occurred just when you thought it should, knowing what you know now, your life could likely have turned out very poorly. Chances are, in retrospect, you're probably happy that several things didn't go exactly as you had originally planned.

The healthy choice is to reflect while you wait. Again, you don't have to look to God for answers while you wait, but the prospects of your other alternatives are not nearly as good. Looking for answers inside yourself, which is quite common, will probably result in things getting worse, especially if you are harboring any guilt from your loss. Seeking help from others certainly has its place; but, you often find that even the wisest people don't have all the answers. Those remedies that they share are not always arranged in a way that works best for you. Sarcastically, I think of waiting on the healing process is much like waiting in line at the motor vehicle department for a new driver's license. It can be an awful experience that exhausts every bit of self-control you can muster; but, just like renewing your driver's license, the consequences of not waiting are likely much worse. Admittedly, if you avoid the wait and take matters into your own hands by immediately stuffing the pain into the busyness of your life or temporarily avoiding the struggle with drugs or alcohol, just like driving without renewing your license, you can likely survive for a while. Ultimately, though, the results of your misguided choice will catch up with you and leave you much worse than had you been more patient.

Another question you may have asked as you wait and reflect is, "How could God possibly have known what he was doing, considering this is the worst thing I can imagine?" I'm not telling you that you'll ever know why you lost your loved one. I believe that you won't until you get to heaven. But, as you heal, if you'll begin to reach outside yourself, you will begin to find healing that at this very moment you probably can't believe even exists, particularly, if you will let others help you first and then transition to reaching out to help others yourself. There is no doubt that in our lives, lots can be learned from suffering. Some very wise people have said that you only learn life's most important lessons through suffering. While that sounds counterintuitive, and none of us would ever go looking for ways to suffer just to be more enlightened, the reality is that it's almost certainly true. J.I. Packer says in Notes From The Valley, "While in suffering, let others take your hand and lead you through."

Interestingly, like it or not, because of your loss, people will be watching to see how you react in this very bad situation. Some people watching will be those who know you because they care about you. Some people will be those who don't know you well, but will be casually be looking for news of how you're doing. And others watching don't know you now, but will find out about how you've dealt with your suffering by talking to some of the people that have watched. Even though right now your spirit may be so weak that you don't want to think or even care about the welfare of others, because you're just trying to survive yourself. Nevertheless, you're being watched. To be clear, I'm not advocating that you try to act a certain way or put on a show because others are observing. It's perfectly all right for you to focus your energy on resetting the compass of your life and you should be doing just that. However, just know that the impact you will have on how other people see God may never be greater than during this period in your life.

Apart from the immeasurable value to yourself, "falling into Jesus" by allowing him to unlock some the answers you need right now in your life, can also inspire positive change in others as they see the way that Christ is giving you strength. What's great about relying on God during this time is the extra benefit you'll get without even trying. As an example, my wife and I have been told by many people over the past few years that they were watching us through our most difficult days, and that they've been amazed and even blessed to see the steadfast nature of our faith. Although several people have told us this, I never cease to be amazed. To some I'm painfully honest and explain that they have no idea how irreverent some of my thoughts about God have been during that time. However, what I've come to appreciate about asking the hard questions about God is that this has probably put me right where He wants me to be, for myself and for others. And as we struggle with God within the context of saying "God I believe in you, but I'm crushed by this outcome and I need you to show me how this makes sense," you're probably going down the road leading to a deeper understanding that is allowing you to gain eternal wisdom that you'll be able to pass along to others. These unintentional, but very valuable insights, are often how others can see growth in our spiritual lives that, in turn, causes them to believe that God really can be the Comforter to the broken-hearted. Amazingly, just the fact that you haven't abandoned God in the most difficult of times is often a huge witness in itself.

14

WHAT REALLY HAPPENS
WHEN PEOPLE DIE?

There are many questions regarding what happens when someone dies that people will say they "sort of knew," but didn't have the occasion to pursue beyond a vague idea. I was one of those people, and quite frankly, I'm certain that a lack of familiarity with some of the specifics of death was a good thing, because it means that I didn't have a pressing need to ever investigate the details. Of course, the time when you begin to want specific answers is usually also connected to examining your own mortality and wondering about the details of a loved one's eternal destination.

C.S. Lewis says, "But either there is 'pie in the sky' or there is not. If there is not (heaven) then Christianity is false, for this doctrine is woven into its whole fabric."

Not being a biblical scholar, I'm hoping that some of the research

I've done for this chapter will save you some time and give you some answers to those numerous questions that may have come to your mind.

*Death: Why do Christians die, especially prematurely?

1. The first and most important thing to know is that God did not cause or allow your loved one's death as a punishment to them or to you for some misbehavior that may have happened. Death is never to be seen as a punishment from God if you're a Christian. The apostle Paul says in Romans 8:1 that there is "no condemnation for those who are in Jesus Christ." Although knowing this to be true is certainly comforting, if we're honest, somewhere in the dark recesses of our minds throughout our lives it's not been unusual to harbor the notion that people eternally get what they deserve, that is, until something happens to us!

2. Good people have died prematurely throughout the ages. Being "good" from a Christian perspective does not necessarily protect people from dying from any variety of causes, including medical complications or accidents of various kinds. Although there are times when God chooses to rescue people from near-death experiences, nowhere in the Bible does He promise to intervene using miraculous circumstances to save people from every occurrence. Instead, death is the natural outcome of humans living in a world that's full of problems. Additionally, God has chosen not to remove all the evil from the world at this time; but instead, He's waiting until some day in the future when we're told there will be a second coming of Christ called the final judgment where all Christians living and dead will be renewed and made perfect, and there will be the establishment of new heavens and a new earth with different rules. The Bible makes it very clear that nobody, except the Father in heaven, knows when this will happen. So, the best way to think of our current circumstances today is that God is waiting

and giving us more time before bringing any final judgment. The Bible teaches that until the second coming of Christ, our experiences are part of a work-in-progress and that God's plan is still incomplete. "The last enemy to be destroyed (by God) is death" (1 Cor. 15:26). Also, an ordained part of our current existence is that Christians, as well as non-Christians, will experience aging, illness, injuries, and natural disasters (such as floods, violent storms, and earthquakes).

3. Death is not always bad … really! Since my son Jared died, I've spent many hours wondering why death should exist at all. In my thinking, I despised the fact that he died young. It felt so unfair. During these times, and since death is painful for so many people, my mind has pondered the question of what possible good could come from death? Further, if it were Adam's original sin that caused death to come into this world, then I'm not sure how allowing the human race to be capable of that type of bad judgment makes any sense either. Surely God saw the original sin coming and could have wired us differently to prevent the whole affair from ever happening which, in my way of thinking, would have kept my son from dying as well. Further, I've wondered how, if God has defeated death through Jesus Christ as we're told as Christians, then why does human death still seem so painful and permanent, and why do I have to live the rest of my life on earth without my son that I loved so much?

With regard to that "wiring issue," theologian Paul Helm says, "The freedom of heaven, then, is the freedom from sin; not that the believer just happens to be free from sin, but that he is so constituted or reconstituted that he cannot sin. He doesn't want to sin, and he does not want to want to sin." Again, the message here is that all the things we think or would like to happen are coming one day for Christians aren't here quite yet.

Of course, questions about "Why Death?" can go on and on, and, to be honest, there are several roads to go down that don't culminate with answers as long as we're on this earth. But, like many "God" things, there are other aspects of death that we do know and can consider. For instance, how many times have you heard people say that it would be merciful if a person with a terminal illness or severe Alzheimer's or a failing body could pass away peacefully. In situations like these, death can be welcomed and even desired as an answer to prayer. So, even though it might not seem this way for you today, even death isn't always bad.

*Heaven: What's It Like and Who Goes There?

The Bible says that the place where God dwells is called heaven. The Bible very specifically teaches that heaven is not just a state of mind, but an actual place and it is located above us. Jesus said, "I go to prepare a <u>place</u> for you" in John 14:2. We know that when Jesus left the earth and was resurrected, he went <u>up</u> into the clouds. So, we are right to think heaven is somewhere above the earth.

If you have just experienced the death of a loved one, regardless of the isolated incidents where death can be a blessing, if you had the chance to take it away permanently, you probably would still be tempted. The apostle John addresses this in *Revelation 21:4* when he writes about the second coming of Christ: "Death shall be no more, neither shall there be mourning, nor crying, not pain anymore, for the former things have passed away." The good news is that it will happen at some point. God guarantees he will kill death at some time in the future. In the meantime, death is significantly different for Christians versus non-Christians. Randy Alcorn writes, "though dying is still difficult for the believer, death itself is radically changed. Death is the means by which God's children enter his presence. Death is not a wall but a turnstile, a last obstacle that marks a great beginning ... For the Christian, death is a difficult means to an incredibly wonderful end."

As we've discussed earlier in this book, while on this earth, Jesus Christ called himself God many times. So, he either was God and all the things he said were true, or he was completely insane and not to be trusted at all! Christ also made it clear that Christians were the ones who could expect heaven after death. Most importantly then, the question should be what does it take to become a Christian? That answer lies unequivocally in this Bible verse: "Jesus answered, 'I am the way the truth and the life. No one comes to the Father (goes to heaven) except through me.'" John 14:6

15

CAN THOSE WHO HAVE
PASSED STILL SEE US? CAN WE
COMMUNICATE WITH THEM?

When I lost my son, to some of my well-meaning friends in an attempt to offer sympathy offered condolences by saying things like, "I know he is looking down on us smiling right now." Unfortunately, this platitude and others that are most certainly made with good intentions likely aren't based on any truth because there is no biblical evidence, or any other evidence for that matter, that a lost loved could be "looking down on us" from a perch in heaven. We do know that heaven fits the definition of paradise, with no pain and no suffering, and lots of fancy stuff like streets of gold and crystal seas. Heaven is described in the Bible as a magnificent place with no worry or heartache. Charles Spurgeon, a great Christian scholar in the 1800s in his "Sermon #2659", describes heaven as a place with no poverty, no toil, no anguish of spirit, no remorse, no struggling with indwelling sin, no battling with foes without or fears within. "They may rest from their labors, for their deeds will follow them." (Revelation 14:13) Spurgeon also said in "Sermon #643" that there are "No Tears in Heaven."

So, if this definition of heaven is true and if your child or loved one could actually look down and see this world with all of its problems, and even see the way you may be feeling right now, how would heaven be anything like paradise? Seemingly, viewing life on earth would be more like watching a scary movie every single day than it would be like living in a place that we're told will be better than our best day on earth!

I'm not implying that God doesn't occasionally gift us with blessings from our loved ones, but they most likely come to us only in the way of fond memories that may feel very near to us in the moment.

Craig Morgan's song "The Father My Son and the Holy Ghost" speaks of those feelings like this:

"But the pain of this was more, than I've ever felt before, yea I was broke. I cried and cried and cried until I passed out on the floor, then I prayed and prayed and prayed until I thought I couldn't pray anymore, then minute by minute and day by day my God, He gave me hope."

Another question that often comes up is: "Where do we go immediately when we die, and how long does it take to get there?" This question usually relates to the concept of purgatory, which is said to be some kind of waiting place to be purged of sins before our final destination. The biblical directive is that there is no delay for judgment and no such place as purgatory. When Jesus died on the cross between two thieves, one scorned him, but the other believed He was the Son of God. Jesus said to that man who believed, *"Today you shall be with me in paradise" (Luke 23:43).* Even though the person Jesus was speaking to had previously been a thief, and was barely even a believer to that point, Jesus specifically said that the man's stated faith that Jesus was the Son of God would cause the man to pass immediately into heaven with no stops! Additionally, there are no other direct references to purgatory in the Protestant canonized Bible (Purgatory is only included in the Catholic canonized Bible).

A similar question regarding the fate of our loved ones is whether or not we should we pray for the dead to assist in determining their final destination. The biblical guidance that the souls of believers go immediately into God's presence means that it would not make sense to pray for the dead after they're gone. Praying for the dead is nowhere taught in the Bible. So, both purgatory and praying for the dead were concepts started by the early Church that have created many conflicts when compared to what the Bible actually tells us about what happens to Christians after death.

Another inquiry that people often make is whether we'll know other people in heaven. Although the Bible does seem to say there will not be marriage in heaven as stated in Matthew 22:30, "At the resurrection people will neither marry nor be given in marriage," which may have some foreshadowing about the concept of our sexual predisposition in heaven. Christianity is the only major religion that believes that you will keep your same identity when you die and go to heaven. In the Bible, when the apostles saw Moses and Elijah appear together with Jesus on a mountainside, they were able to identify them, even though they had been dead for many years. We don't have a lot of other guidance in this area. The Bible talks about our spiritual bodies and our physical bodies but doesn't make precise distinctions about the state of these after we die.

C.S. Lewis has said this about our spiritual bodies: "I agree that we don't know what a spiritual body is. But I don't like contrasting it with 'an actual, physical body.' This suggests that the spiritual body would be the opposite of 'actual' – i.e., some kind of vision or imagination. And I do think most people imagine it as something that looks like the present body and isn't really there. Our Lord's eating the boiled fish (when Jesus appeared after he rose from the dead) seems to put the boots to that idea, don't you think? I suspect the distinction is the other way around – that it is something compared with which our present bodies are half real and phantasmal."

Religions, such as Buddhism, Hinduism, and New Age mysticism, believe we will be spiritually anonymous. These religions teach that individuality is obliterated or just assimilated into a state they would call nirvana. For me, heaven would be difficult to aspire to if we were all strangers with no ability to reacquaint with others, which also would seem to include having distinctives about a person, like features, memory, personality, gifts, passions, and interests. Most all non-Christian faiths believe that those distinctions will all be gone after a person dies. The view that our lives in heaven will have no characteristics or attachment to our current lives doesn't seem to me to be appealing.

The last significant thing to know about what happens to Christians after we die is that we're told that even the existing heaven is not our final destination. In the Bible, God promises that when Jesus returns to the earth a second time, it will lead to the ultimate creation of a new heaven and new earth where we will live. Many think that when this happens, it will again be like the garden of Eden where all things are "good" and people will live forever. Additionally, the narrative says that we will somehow again re-inherit our earthly bodies, but that this time they'll be perfect. Of course, this brings up other questions, like what if we had physical limitations here on earth, how will we be recognizable to each other in heaven or on the new earth without those issues? To me, those issues will become very inconsequential if we're living in paradise! The point is that even though heaven has some attributes we can know about now, our destination on the new earth has many details that we're just not privileged to know at this time.

Just knowing that I will recognize my son when I see him again in heaven is enough to want to pursue the God who makes that part of the plan! Best of all, it seems to me that an attractive benefit to understanding the Bible is that this kind of knowledge is an incentive for people to want to find out more about the God who is making those promises!

16

⟵ ✴ ⟶

HOW SHOULD I BE ACTING
THROUGH ALL OF THIS?

"*How many times you make the waves calm down, so I won't be afraid.*" "*I saw you breaking my fall, what am I supposed to do?*" *Breaking My Fall – Jeremy Camp*

After a tragedy like losing a loved one, it's not uncommon to feel like you're living in a fog where everything feels heavy and hard as if you're in a bad dream. During those times, I found myself wishing I could wake up, have my son back and well again, and resume as normal. Having been a very action-oriented person my whole life and never being one to hesitate to work hard for the things I wanted to achieve, the helplessness was difficult for me to accept. Unfortunately, my inability to make sense of everything just led to additional frustration as if I were walking in the dark.

The longer you focus on the problem and the more you try to resolve it in your mind, the worse it seems to get. At this point, when you feel there's no place to go, it's not unusual to start looking for an outlet to expend this bottled-up energy. For me, this anxiousness got really bad at the hospital, knowing they were about to turn off my son's ventilator and realizing he wouldn't last long thereafter. I asked one of our pastor friends who had come up to be with us, "How am I supposed to act through all this? What should I be feeling? What should I be saying in these moments?" I can remember having that sinking feeling the entire time that comes when you've taken a wrong turn and find yourself lost in an unfamiliar place; however, in this case, I was standing right there with all my family and friends.

The response I received to my question, in retrospect, was the best I could get; but, truthfully in moments like that, there are no "right" answers. He explained to me that I didn't have to act any certain way and that I didn't owe a certain response to anyone during that time. As I said, certainly that advice is acceptable, and frankly, there is almost nothing a person could do in those moments that isn't excusable, considering the circumstances. My point is that, as much as you'd like someone to help you make the unresolved anxiety go away, there is no way to behave that is any better than another. Although I wanted to draw my friends and family close, I equally wanted to go outside and run away from the hospital and never look back.

C. S. Lewis described the feeling this way in A Grief Observed: "At other times it feels like being mildly drunk, or even concussed. There is a sort of invisible blanket between the world and me. I find it hard to take in what anyone says. Or perhaps, hard to want to take it in. It is so uninteresting. Yet I want the others about me. I dread the moments when the house is empty. If only they would talk to one another and not to me ... An odd by-product of my loss is that I'm aware of being an embarrassment to everyone I meet. At work, at the club, in the street, I see people, as they approach me, trying to make up their minds whether they'll 'say something about it' or not. I hate if they do, and if they don't."

It would be nice to offer more helpful information on this subject;

but, following your instincts regarding what seems best for the situation in that moment is probably the best advice anyone can give. All I would say is that I tried to make an effort to appreciate the people that came around and were there to help knowing they had the best intentions, or they wouldn't have come. Try to remember they're your family or friends and treating them rudely just because you feel awful won't help anything. Remember what the situation would be like if you had come to help a friend under the same circumstances and how difficult it can be to know what to do when you wanted to help.

17

————— ❦ —————

WAS THIS MY FAULT?

E mpathy is the ability to share and understand the thoughts and feelings of others. I've never been very good at connection with people's feelings but sometimes I feel like I understand their thoughts, even though with some differentiating between the two can be difficult. It seems that for some people, thoughts and feelings can be almost the same, and in others like me, feelings can be much different than thoughts. For instance, when my son died, I felt like I could barely breathe and that I would have liked to curl up in a ball and lie in the corner, which I know some people have done. However, my thoughts told me I needed to be strong for my family and that I needed to try to keep trying to move forward so I didn't do something that would cause others to struggle or that I'd regret later, so that's what I did. In addition, my thoughts told me that curling up in a ball wasn't really going to make me feel better, so, why bother.

In the case of my son's passing, it has been interesting to find out that many people have had personal struggles because they've somehow blamed themselves for the tragedy, even though no one could have known to act differently to prevent Jared's death. It is shocking that my wife, my son, his girlfriend, his grandparents, some of his friends, and I have all have expressed feelings of guilt about what happened—all from different points of view.

How absurd is that? Several people blaming themselves for the same event all at once! Of course, logically, it couldn't have possibly been everyone's fault, and the reality was that it wasn't the fault of any of us! But, strangely, somehow, we allowed ourselves to be convicted by thoughts that weren't true, and in some cases found ourselves even momentarily struggling with the convoluted lies we had conjured up. The worst part of this whole picture is how self-absorbed this shows we can become, as if any of us were so influential to God that our guilt, shameful behavior, lack of faith or whatever else, could be the reason He would exchange my son's life to resolve our mistakes! In times like this, it's often good to have someone to remind us gently that, although unintended, we've become so blinded to our standing with God that we have convinced ourselves that we're the reason that something like this would really happen. Regardless, it can still be human nature for people close to tragedy to wonder if they are somehow at fault for the tragedy and if there were something they should have done differently to keep it from happening. Usually that "thing" is perceived to be some type of personal sin or misbehavior.

18

———— ❦ ————

WHAT IF MY SPOUSE AND I GRIEVE THIS LOSS DIFFERENTLY? WHO'S RIGHT? IS THERE A "RIGHT"?

Another common regret of those close to someone that has died is lamenting that, had they known, they would have said or done something more while they were alive or at least have another chance to say goodbye. When these thoughts come to you, I would challenge you not to allow yourself to hit the dead end that comes from wishing for something that you know can't happen, even though your heart wants it more than anything in the world. Instead, try to replace the pain of your loss by considering your spouse and your friends and expressing what they mean to you. Attempt to start to look at the others around you at the hospital or your home, and to realize that they are probably hurting just like you are. Although, in these moments, it's understandable to feel like you're the only one affected by the pain; but instead, try to consider ways that you might reach out to others.

By empathizing with their feelings and by becoming approachable, they may feel comfortable sharing their sorrows with you. Carefully ask them about the guilt they may be experiencing and help them recognize that those feelings aren't true and that they needlessly add more pain to an already-painful situation. Strangely, knowing that other people are hurting around you and choosing to come alongside them as a comforter can become a game changer for you personally as well. Prompt yourself to use your shared pain as an invitation to pour words of healing into others, which will miraculously allow you to feel the weight of sorrow being lifted from you as you speak! Both now and as you continue to climb out of what feels like a deep well of grief, from my experience the secret to finding the healing you're looking for is not to just hope for your circumstances to change, even though that is a very tempting to do. Instead, a way to receive the most relief from grief and suffering is to look beyond your own pain and provide aid for the grief of others. Unfortunately, I'm not that kind of person, and I had to be very intentional about reaching out and connecting with others. By the way, I realize that it's still critical that you should find time for yourself, and it's also necessary to let yourself grieve in the way that makes sense to you. For me, I find that having a good cry, while maybe not being very masculine, has been extremely cleansing for my pain. However, aside from necessary times of introspection, ultimately getting your mind off your own despair and investing in the healthy outlet of reaching into the lives of the others hurting around you, will help you steer clear of the dangerous times when you can go spinning down the drain of personal despair. I truly believe that reaching out to others is the best start toward filling that massive hole that's now inside of you. Really! I challenge you to try it! I'll think you'll be extremely surprised by the good results.

You may have heard that it's extremely common for the loss of a child to cause the break-up of marriages at an extremely alarming level. While some experts have recently said that the actual number of divorces due to child loss is more urban legend than actual fact, you may have still been bothered by the fact that your husband or wife is handling the grieving process differently than you are. While it feels strange and can certainly lead to relational tension, it turns out this occurrence is very normal. Grieving problems that strain relationships typically occur when one person doesn't believe that their mate is grieving "right," "enough" or "in a healthy way." When people's emotions are understandably strained, it doesn't take much of a disagreement between married partners to ignite some fireworks that can pit them against each other. Small issues can easily turn into large conflicts and people can become convinced they won't ever again be capable of getting along. Additionally, married partners may find out that their focused love for their children, or increased dedication to the management of the family, has replaced their love for their spouse, which can leave their personal relationship feeling hollow.

In these times, humility needs to be the order of the day. It's been said that the proud person asks, "Why me?" but that the humble person says, "Why not me?" Steve Leder, the Jewish rabbi, writes, "Do you want to heal painful wounds in your friendships and family? Then inject some doubt into your self-righteousness. Only doubt enables us to consider, maybe it's me. Maybe she is right. Maybe he does have a point. Maybe I was unkind. Maybe I was too severe, insecure, self-righteous, proud, aggressive. Maybe I was wrong." While I certainly understand that asking more of yourself when you've just experienced the biggest gut punch of your life may seem very difficult, consider that the quality of the rest of your life on this earth may pivot on your actions over the next weeks and months. Even though it might feel justified, I would encourage you not to allow your pain to be the reason for treating others without compassion. This may be a time you have to force yourself to realize that there is no sense in making a bad situation worse.

For me, my wife and I heard early on that the best defense against a break-up was just committing ourselves to giving one another space and vocalizing to each other that we weren't going to let this awful event come between us. In times of non-conflict, just being aware that you may soon be mightily tested is a great way to stand together in this tough time.

Next, we found it important to find a strategy that can be your default when you feel that things may be heading south. Decide that if you feel tension, you will do something to help yourself to regain perspective. Go for a walk, have a good memory to bring up and share, or just hold each other and don't say anything when tensions are high. It's best to have a dependable failsafe, because circumstances can often become volatile. The key is to find whatever you know works for you and that you can trust your mate to do well, even when you may not feel like working things through.

Early on, my wife and I spent lots of time remembering people we knew whose relationships had been blown apart by the death of a child and we committed ourselves not to let it happen to us. We verbalized our commitment to stay together and we prayed that God would have mercy on us to continue to get along.

Please don't get the impression that the plan of action I'm recommending is easy. I know from experience that it is not. My wife is a completely different personality type than I am, and we often see things very differently. In the months and years since we lost our son, I've figured out that I have a much more analytical view about suffering and loss and my wife is much more emotion-driven. For my wife, dealing with grief has meant staying focused on managing her personal feelings and acting on what her emotions tell her about her condition. Consequently, while she still struggles with her wounded heart over and over, she hasn't been inclined to ask God why the event happened; but rather, is more likely to ask, "why do I feel this emptiness?" and "when is it going to end?" She will often find herself wanting to shoulder some sort of blame for losing our son, rather than being tempted to blame anyone else or God. In reading this book, you know what I've been doing with my grief energy and I'm hoping that you can gain insight from both of our approaches.

19

———— ❧ ————

CAN CHRISTIANITY GIVE
ME COMFORT IN THIS?

I t often becomes clear with the death of a child or loved one that involves immense suffering and grief that we must acknowledge, possibly for the first time, that we will not achieve the life of stability and comfort that we may have always thought we would. While this sensation of instability quickly becomes apparent and obvious, the next move in life is seldom clear. You must either decide to approach the time you have left on earth using your own strength and form your own plan, or to look to God or something else to provide the compass for your direction forward. If you chose the spiritual route, you realize that the ultimate goal for your earthly existence is tied to a time after your life on earth, which for Christians, involves the expectation of heaven.

After my 20-year-old son unexpectedly died, I found myself in disbelief of my circumstances, and although I never felt that God had abandoned me, I certainly wasn't at all happy with the way He seemed to have handled things. Honestly, why should I have been? As a result of being a Christian most of my life, and because I am a very practical person, I realized my other alternatives were mostly all bad outside of pursuing God for answers. So, I decided I was going to study, read, and talk to Godly people to find out everything I could about how my view of God must be flawed so that I could continue as a believer the rest of my life.

As I said, although the death of my son Jared didn't destroy my foundational belief in the sovereignty of God, it did require that I rebuild the house that sits on top of that foundation so to speak. One of those rebuilding plans has been to investigate the verses in the Bible that seem to say the exact opposite of what I experienced in my life. For instance, John 14:13 says "Whatever you shall ask in my name, that will I do." And Luke 11:10 says, "For everyone that asks receives." There are many more. For those of us who don't have every verse in the Bible committed to memory, we probably have read or heard similar verses and wondered why they seem so opposite of our reality! Has God been taunting us, or even worse?

If pressed, you likely already realize that these verses don't translate literally to what we think we hear when we read them. Even though they may sound like we can ask for anything and a genie in the bottle will appear to grant our wish, that can't be the meaning! Of course, if that is what they really meant, all Christians would be rich and famous and everything in our lives would always go well. However, the reality is that even for God's own son, Jesus, seldom did things go smoothly. Even as he neared death, Jesus asked for this earthly "cup" to be taken from him, which meant to keep him from suffering and dying on a wooden cross. But that's exactly what happened! In addition, nearly all of Jesus' own disciples, including the apostle Paul, were martyred for their faith, as were the Old Testament prophets who died for their faith as well!

So, what about these verses? Are they saying that they hold no meaning at all or that they cannot be tied to only things on earth?

Oswald Chambers in *My Utmost for His Highest* writes that Jesus is talking about "God things" and not necessarily things of this life. So, the question becomes, Are "God things" completely the opposite of human things, and if so, what's the point?

C.S. Lewis asks the question this way in his book, "The Problem of Pain": The word good, applied to Him, becomes meaningless, like abracadabra. We have no motive for obeying Him. Not even fear. It is true we have His threats and promises. But why should we believe them? If cruelty is from His point of view 'good,' telling lies may be 'good' too. Even if they are true, what then? If His ideas of good are so very different from ours, what He calls Heaven might well be what we call Hell and vice-versa."

This can also cause you to wonder if this means that things of this life don't count at all, but if they still do, how much?

From what I've come to understand, the answer is that this life does matter, even as it influences the bigger picture, which includes life after death or eternity. Although some Bible verses can be difficult to understand or apply to a certain context if taken by themselves, what we find out from several other verses is that God indeed does care about what goes on in this life. What we say and do and what other people say and do influence the bigger picture. The tough part is framing the specific meaning in the way it was intended and not just relying on our limited perspective. For instance, as a parent, how many times did you tell your child to do something or not to do something where the results of that instruction weren't immediately obvious to them? Likely many times! Because of your superior wisdom as a parent, you knew how those instructions would ultimately work themselves out in time. Depending on the circumstances, sometimes you explained your response, but also insisted that the request you made of your child be carried out, but sometimes not. Even with your limited view of the future, you knew what the results would be like of a specific action because of your experience in similar situations. If we consider that God can see all time and has infinitely more wisdom that we have, then why wouldn't we understand that "good" in Romans 8:28, "God works all things for good for those who love him" doesn't mean that "good" isn't still good, but only that the timeframe to become good must be greatly outside of our limited perspective?

If this all seems too cliché for you, consider the assumed concept that if God is God, he would have ultimate wisdom. At last count there were 7.8 billion people on the planet, and it would be expected that God, as much as we can understand an omnipotent God, would know everything about all of them, which the Bible says that he does. Every hair on each head, so to speak. By the way, it makes sense that this includes believers in God and even nonbelievers as well. Also, God says he created all the plants, animals, and planets, etc., and everything we don't see, like atoms and molecules as well. God says he knows everything about all those things from the past, present and future. Based on that kind of knowledge, if anyone tries telling you they can really comprehend God's prerogatives, meaning what God should or shouldn't do to manage all those things at any point in time, you can easily surmise that they have no idea what they're talking about! With this thought-provoking perspective in mind that God knows everything, you must then assume that God knows about you, and your loss, and the suffering that you're experiencing now, but also what your life looks like down the road as well.

"There are, aren't there, only three things we can do about death: to desire it, to fear it, or to ignore it. The third alternative, which is the one the modern world calls 'healthy' is surely the most uneasy and precarious of all." C. S. Lewis from a Letter to Mary Willis Shelbourne

There is no question that in your lifetime the loss you may have recently experienced will always be a source of pain. Sometimes more acute than others. However, letting that hurt cripple your other responsibilities to yourself and the people around you, and even to those you don't know yet but might have the opportunity to help someday, isn't likely what you really want for your life, nor is it what God wants for you. Don't get me wrong, I'm still advocating taking the time to grieve, and heal, and grieve, and heal some more. But my advice beyond that is to pursue healing by focusing on helping others and not allowing yourself to dive so deeply into your own pain that you can't swim back to the top. If you'll remember those things, you'll very likely find that God will gladly provide you the peace you're looking for a moment at a time.

When people first start to pursue God in earnest, they often soon find out that neither Christianity nor the Bible offers a full explanation of God's reasons for allowing the existence of death, evil, and suffering aside from a view back to the first sin on earth. And although that lack of information can seem frustrating when you'd prefer something more personal, Christianity provides the final answer to the mysteries of our current existence, which, as it turns out, are as much about achieving a spiritual eternal existence as they are about our current physical one.

One of C.S. Lewis famous lines about the spiritual side of life is "the doors of hell are locked from the inside." That can be a very interesting thought if you consider the situation that analogy describes. It's been my experience that much of the healing that God can offer to those who have lost loved ones is contingent on just how much, and in what way, we open the doors of our lives to be available for healing. The understandable anxiety, frustration, and even anger with God for allowing something so bad to happen, and especially something that doesn't seem right or fair, is the same set of emotions that can continue to keep the doors of your heart and mind locked from the inside for healing as well. In moments of failure, frustration, and grief, we all feel alone and abandoned. It's easy to wonder where God is in those moments. However, the reality, that doesn't seem like reality, is that God is right there next to you, and He's seeing what you're seeing and feeling what you're feeling. Again, in this world, God has not promised our lives will be without struggles. We all know this to be true even though we mostly don't want to think about those times because we know they will be negative. As we experience the pain suffered in our own lives, it's important to remember that God promises "He will never leave you or forsake you." Deuteronomy 31:8

Like a lot of other perplexing "God things," the process of healing isn't immediate and comes over time from what God does from inside you. It also isn't usually an external change of your circumstances by God reducing the stresses in the environment around you. If you've ever slammed a door in anger, you can picture figuratively what is happening in your heart when you're mad at God. I'm not inferring that I wasn't mad at God when my son died—I was. Real mad for a time! When my son died, I felt like I was falling down a deep well and was quickly approaching hitting the bottom. Miraculously, I ultimately did feel as though God had a long rope around me as I fell that kept me from splattering on the bottom, I was figurately still kicking and screaming at God the whole way down. Once I neared the bottom, which was delayed by having all my family and friends around for the funeral and busying myself with the logistics of taking care of the postmortem details, somehow, I knew that the only way out of the deep hole was to reach out my hand by seeking the answers about God that served as rungs of the ladder that would help me to climb out. The decision to pursue God and not to abandon Him was certainly the fork in the road for me. Because I'm stubborn, instead of just allowing God to guide my feet onto those steps of the ladder and make the healing easier, I took the hard way by working to prove to myself why God had either caused or allowed this awful thing to happen. My thought was that in order to redevelop my trust in God I needed to find some answers to my many "why" questions. As a result, I began pursuing those answers through reading, researching, talking to people, praying, and studying.

In my quest to learn to trust God again by seeking understanding about my son's death, I've discovered some good news and some bad news. The bad news is, as I've already told you, there are some significant answers to fairly common questions that it appears we won't understand in this lifetime. However, the good news is that there are more satisfying answers available than you might think! Where this gets complex is that some of the available answers are logical and have tangible parts to them so they will bring you some immediate understanding. However, some of the answers, as you've probably discovered in reading this book, are going to force you to pull your guard down, humbly change your perspective, and force you to search your inner self on issues that defy standard logic and reason. For people like me, this can be the part that's really tough. Due to these complexities, I've been forced to say, "All right, God, somehow I'm going to attempt to follow a plan for my life that's on your terms and not mine." Once you make that commitment and release some of the doubt and anger, your perspective will start to take on a whole new outlook. Don't get me wrong, the hurt will never completely go away, not now, and likely, not ever. However, the waves of pain and grief that break on your emotional shores will occur less frequently as time goes on. For me, one way healing has occurred is when God has occasionally allowed me to strangely feel like I'm viewing my life from outside myself, allowing me a different perspective than what I see in the here and now. When this sporadically happens, it's as if I'm "peeking behind the curtain" so to speak, which helps me to get the sense that there is much more to this existence than what meets the eye. Interestingly, the more I know about God and his ways, which includes how the spiritual side of our existence intersects with the physical of our lives on the earth, the more I understand these "other-worldly visions" that bring encouragement and great hope for the eternal.

One very significant element that I've gained from my grief study is that when you compare all the major world religions, Christianity is the only one that gives a fulfilling view of what happens after we die, assuming we genuinely believe in Jesus as our God.

*"And on that day when my strength is fading, the end is near and my time has come, still my soul will sing your praise unending, 10,000 years and then forever more ... forever more!!" *Bless The Lord Oh My Soul (10,000 Reasons)*

If you aren't familiar with why we should put our faith in Jesus during the hardest of times, here's a fast refresher. In John 14:20, Jesus says, "My Father and I are one." Here Jesus is saying that he is GOD! Also, in John 10:32 Jesus asks some bad people, "For what sin are you attempting to kill me?" Basically, Jesus is saying that He is perfect! Interestingly, there has never been a leader of any world religion that has said he's God or that he's perfect except Jesus. So, despite when people today say that Jesus was just another good man or a good teacher, etc., that can't be true! Either he was the most disturbed leader ever and not to be trusted in anything, or he was who he said he was! You can't say you're God and not be God, but assume anything else you say has any credibility! So, if it is true, and when Jesus walked the earth, he was fully God and, of course, he was also a man, then the Bible is true. And the best part is, if the Bible is the true story of God, then we really do have a place we can go to look for answers when we're in a dark place of pain and suffering. And by diving deeply into the words of the Bible, we're very likely to find the prescription to make it through to tomorrow, and the next day, and the day after that, even though we're feeling greater pain than we've ever felt before.

Strangely, even though God created us, we're free to dismiss Him over issues that we disagree with him on, like allowing great tragedy in our lives. However, if we do, what is the alternative? We can look to our own sensibilities, but those can seem hauntingly empty when it comes to the really tough questions. We can lean on other people, but do we really trust that others have the solutions to our problems? As we've explored, these might even be the same people who avoid discussing our loss because they don't know what to say or want to avoid an uncomfortable topic. We can resort to artificial stimulants like alcohol and drugs, but they are obviously temporary, and most often leave us worse than before we started. The best part is, if you pursue God, you'll one day see how the whole picture of your life fits together and somehow makes sense. When that day comes, your joy will be complete, and all your hurt will go away. For now, persevere faithfully!

"Remember, He hasn't forgotten that one of the special people that called him "Daddy" is no longer around to do it. Tell him you remember, too. Speak His child's name and share a special memory."

Unknown

20

———— ✣ ————

WHAT AM I SUPPOSED TO DO NOW?

How do you move forward? As you may have reasoned from other circumstances, oftentimes results depend on your expectations at the outset. The very old adage, "You can see the glass half full or half empty," sounds cliché, but it can be very true. Grief creates a very negative perception of life for the short term that often spills over into the long term as well. After loss, the majority of our lives are still mostly intact in the big picture, although I certainly understand it doesn't feel that way! However, with some refocusing, we can force ourselves to be thankful for the things we still have, like our home, food, and friends and family that care about us, etc. Without making this seem too simple, the beginning of the pathway out of the downward emotional cycle is pulling together all the energy you can muster and force yourself to see the good things around you. Start with a few simple things so it won't feel too contrived, and then add one item at a time to your mental blessing inventory whenever necessary.

I can attest from my own experience that there will almost certainly be times of backsliding. Certainly, grieving and processing the specific thoughts that are tied to your pain are healthy to do and also necessary. Having time to picture your loved one, to reflect on their face, and to hear their voice is what your heart and mind will go to frequently, and there is absolutely nothing wrong with that and you should allow yourself to go there. However, in between the waves of grief, which is the most descriptive way to explain the experience, it will help if you exercise as much self-control as possible to focus on the blessings you still have in your life. Acting on this gratitude by verbalizing the things you're thankful for to the people around you that are trying to help is an excellent way gradually to help pull yourself up from the depths of your despair. Additionally, although reaching out to others that are hurting and encouraging them to do the same may feel like it will deplete what little energy you have left, it will instead likely help you to feel stronger and reward you for your efforts!

One of the most thought-provoking things about the recovery process is something I read from the Jewish rabbi Steve Leder. He says that "most people would say that 'life is short, you have to make the most of it!' I would remind them that life is long. Long enough to start again, to rebuild, to take more pictures, to create more memories, to heal."

As I mentioned earlier, if you've lost a child or someone very close to you, it isn't unusual that before long others who know about your loss will call on you to talk with people who have also recently lost loved ones. When I've had this opportunity and people have asked me the question "what am I supposed to do now," I remind them of a truth that helped me get through that very difficult time. It often seems like our lives are divided almost like a book into chapters or stages that include related events that become all-consuming for us at any single point in time. If you have lost a child or a spouse, one of those chapters has just begun very abruptly. However, the important thing to remember is that before you were a parent, or before you were married, or before you knew that friend, you had a life and an identity that was equally as important during that chapter as the other chapters that included the person that you've lost. While it's not your choice now, you must remember that your loved one was only a part of your life for a time, but not your whole life. For instance, they may have been a member of your family, but they were not your entire family. God put you on this earth not only to be their parent, spouse or friend, but also to be available to others and for many other important reasons that you may not even know yet. When you're ready, it will be your responsibility to dig down and find the part of you that still has a separate purpose and an identity that is not tied specifically to ones you've loved and lost.

This approach doesn't mean you have to or want to or will ever forget those chapters of your life that included your loved one. However, just as other significant events in your life have changed your trajectory, this one will as well. Now it's your responsibility to search out the positives and not allow only the negatives to dominate your worldview. Fortunately, all the blessings and enhancements to your character that you gained by knowing that person don't have to be wasted. If those people were still around, they certainly wouldn't want you to throw away those positive attributes, would they? However, it's up to you to be intentional about taking what you've learned from having life experiences with that person and allowing them to propel you to the next level. A similar example would be utilizing the wisdom and knowledge you've gained from doing another job or occupation to help you excel in the things you're doing now.

As we've discussed, when you've lost a loved one, many of your friends will feel uncomfortable talking to you about your feelings in the same way that you may have felt uncomfortable with others you've wanted to console in the past. People often assume that speaking of that person will only remind you of the bad memories of losing that the person, when, in reality, talking about your loved one can be therapeutic and a good way to help you process your grief. If your friends are bold enough to ask about how you're doing or what they can do to help, you may want to consider some things ahead of time that you can say that will include talking about ways they remember your loved one. Because I'm often thinking ahead, somehow, I knew that things would get harder after the funeral was over and when the commotion subsided from my son's death. That expectation allowed me to be ready when some of my close friends asked what they could do to help. I said, "I'm going to need your help in making it through this weeks and years from now when most people no longer want to think about this anymore. Please don't forget to talk with me about Jared and remind me of all the great things about him. I might cry, but it will be a good cry." Thankfully, several of those friends have taken me at my word and are still helping me now years later!

Lastly, I want to leave you with this: Because of my son's faith and my faith in God and in the message of the Bible, I believe there is a day coming where I'll be reunited with my son, and the reason God permitted him to unexpectedly leave this earth when he was only 20 years old will finally make sense to me. This Bible verse describes for me what that day will be like when it all will be clear, and all the questions and pain will be swallowed up in an overwhelming sense of peace. I believe that these words contain the real answer on how to process the "why" questions that you may have had before reading this book:

Jesus says in John 16:22-23, "Now is your time of grief, but I will see you again, and you will rejoice, and no one will take away your joy. In that day you will ask Me nothing."

I pray for you this hope as well!

BIBLIOGRAPHY

J.I. Packer, *Evangelism and the Sovereignty of God*, (InterVarsity Press, England, 1961)

C.S. Lewis, *A Grief Observed*, (New York: Harper Collins, 1961)

C.S. Lewis, *The Problem Of Pain*, (New York: Harper Collins, 1940)

Philip Yancy, *Disappointment with God*, (Grand Rapids, Michigan: Zondervan Publishing House, 1988)

Randy Alcorn, *We Shall See God*, (Carol Stream, Illinois: Tyndale House Publishers, Inc., 2011)

Timothy Keller, *Walking with God through Pain and Suffering*, (New York; Penguin Random House, 2013)

Steve Leder, *More Beautiful Than Before*, (Carlsbad, California, New York City, London, Sydney, New Delhi; Hay House Inc., 2017)

Oswald Chambers, *My Utmost For His Highest*, (Grand Rapids, Michigan: Discovery House Publishers, 1935)

Andy McQuitty, *Notes from the Valley,* (Chicago, Illinois: Moody Publishers, 2015)

Wayne Grudem, *Bible Doctrine,* (Grand Rapids, Michigan: Zondervan, 1999)

Jonathan Foster, *Where Was God On The Worst Day of My Life,* (Jonathan J. Foster, 2015)

Paul Helm, *The Last Things* (Carlisle, PA; Banner of Truth, 1989)

New Revised Standard Edition Bible, *The C.S. Lewis Bible* (HarperOne, 1st edition, 2010)

HERE IS HOW YOU CAN
HELP OTHERS

Dear Reader,

If you don't currently know of others that are hurting and grieving today, you likely will before long. There is something simple you can do to help them and that is to leave a short review of this book on Amazon. Just search for the *"Why God?"* Brave Questions That Need Answers After Suffering Loss book on Amazon and page down to "Customer Reviews" on the left side and click on "Write a Review". By doing this it will allow others to find this book when searching words like "loss", "grief" or "suffering", since the algorithms that run these searches are based on popularity and on number of reviews.

Thanks for considering this and I will look forward to reading your review as well.

Thank you!
Darren

CONTACT THE AUTHOR

Darren Frame is interested in helping as many people as possible with the material contained in this book. He offers himself to anyone who is dealing with grief and loss or those seeking to help others.

As a capable speaker and communicator, Darren is available to do public presentations for various venues and audiences.

To book an appointment email <u>DF@MarshallResources.com</u> or call 480-998-4279 and leave a message.

Printed in the United States
by Baker & Taylor Publisher Services